THE GREAT POSSUM-SQUASHING AND BEER STORM OF 1962

THE GREAT POSSUM-SQUASHING AND BEER STORM OF 1962

REFLECTIONS ON THE REMAINS OF MY COUNTRY

Fred Reed

Writers Club Press

San Jose New York Lincoln Shanghai

The Great Possum-Squashing and Beer Storm of 1962
Reflections on the Remains of My Country

Writers Club Press
an imprint of iUniverse.com, Inc.

For information address:
iUniverse.com, Inc.
5220 S 16th, Ste. 200
Lincoln, NE 68512
www.iuniverse.com

ISBN: 0-595-15109-4

Printed in the United States of America

To Macon Elizabeth and Emily Anne, the smartest, prettiest, and most intractable girl-children of which any father was ever blessed to be, briefly, the proprietor.

Foreword

Late night in August of 1999, maybe three a.m. on Washington's belt-way, in a buddy's male-menopause red Miata. Top down, revs up. Rock'n'roll from 1964 squalled from the speakers. The highway stretched away before us, as dark and empty as an anchorman's mind. I was three sheets to the wind on Bud, and undergoing a Life Change. Big time.

Having spent most of my working years in the newspaper colum-nist's dismal trade, I had just decided to bail out of serious journalism, if indeed it was, and betake myself to the Web. It was either that or get my duck gun and begin shooting city editors. The choice was more dif-ficult than you might have expected.

After 26 years, I was weary of the news racket. I'd enjoyed it for a while. Privilege without responsibility is heady stuff. But the fun had gone out of it. Journalism in general had come to have the appeal of a moist skin disease, but wasn't as much fun to scratch. Newspapers were worst, except for television, which apparently gets its employees from another phylum.

The papers were intellectually equivalent to the underside of a the-ater seat. To be fair (which I try to avoid doing) newspapers weren't bad, provided that one were willing to write without wit, intelligence, thought, honesty, knowledge, comprehension, style, or recognizable grammar. But I wasn't. And newspapers were tightly censored by that vague but rigid control we call political correctness. Writers had all become flacks for a gelatinous adolescent philosophy that didn't really have a name.

We were frauds. The writers that editors refer to as archetypes of the trade—Mencken, Twain, Bierce, Ernie Pyle—could not today be published. All would instantly be charged with sexism, racism, date rape, child molestation, and insensitivity to the variegated tribes of human parsnips whom we are today expected to take seriously.

Further, newspapermen themselves had gone to hell. Once a fraternity of honest drunks, they had become snotty Ivy League delicates, well-groomed things who looked gender-puzzled even in a fern bar. Real reporters gazed at them in sorrow and figured they needed mulching. I missed the old school—the cynical, boisterously obscene, ashen-souled, hard-drinking, harder-nosed, chain-smoking, blasphemous, irreverent, and courageous men found in the press bars of Nairobi and Saigon.

I mean, God almighty: a *police reporter* from *Harvard*?

And the truth wasn't in them. Granted, journalism has never been quite as consumed with seeking the truth as it likes to pretend. Somebody owns the paper and has certain, usually Republican, views. The reporters are Democrats. Certain compromises have always followed. But something worse has happened now. When reporters know the truth, they repress it. We all know what we have to say. Consequently what reporters know, they don't say, and what they say, they don't believe. And, dear god, the piety, the solemnity, the self-infatuation, and the sentence structure.

I fled.

I decided that I would invent a Web column, and see whether anyone would read it. If they didn't, well, they didn't. I could always go to live in the red-light district of Bangkok. But a Web-only column would be an adventure. The Web was uncharted territory, a journalistic Dodge City. I'd write what the hell I pleased. The advertisers could be damned, since I didn't have any. The real clue to the wisdom of the undertaking would be whether I got lynched. If not, I would collect my ravings in a book, and sell that sucker. And if I was lynched, well, better to be a dead Twain than a living Goebbels.

I did write the column, and called it Fred On Everything, so as not unduly to limit my scope. To my gratification, people do read the beast, in growing numbers. As time went by, thousands subscribed. People forwarded the rascal all over the face of the earth. (You can find it at www.FredOnEverything.net) I didn't get lynched, though it was a near thing, and so I stuffed all the first year's columns into a book, and you're holding it. I hope you like reading it as much as I liked writing it.

Contents

1

Harassing General Claudia

Why me, oh Lord? Doesn't Job handle the really awful tribulations?

The other day I picked up a newspaper and found, page one, above the fold, that a three-star generalette in the Army, name of Claudia Kennedy, has her skivvies in a knot. It's because an unnamed he-general groped her years ago. Yep, he did. She says.

Or maybe he patted her on the fanny, or looked at her, or made her uncomfortable, like a lint-ball in a sock. The newspapers weren't real clear on this. They are, after all, newspapers.

This, I sensed, was a military story of vast importance, like Pearl Harbor.

I tried to get my mind around it: Yet another installment of the Great Pentagonal Grope'n'Squeal shriek-he-touched-me sex-harassment-is-everywhere sit-com. More and sillier charges. Angry fluttering in the hencoop. Roosters running for cover.

I'm telling you, reality gets harder to grab hold of every hour.

All right, I figured. Maybe it was a slow day in the newsroom. Maybe, in fact, a day that was actually dead, and waiting to be stuffed: Nothing at all to write about. You can't put out a blank paper. Thus a harrowing tale of unsuccessful rutting on the E-Ring. Whoopee.

I forgot about it.

Next day, so help me, another page-one piece: *They had discovered the identity of the groper.* Yes, there he was. Guy named Larry Smith. This revelation was treated as a great astonishment, as if the press had found Clinton in bed with his wife. The obvious question—"Who cares?"—eluded capture.

Now, why do you think Kennedy (whom some now call Attila the Hen) is doing this? She's likely to destroy the guy's career, heterosexuality being in disrepute in the military, and she knows it. Groped? At her age you'd think she'd be grateful. Do we have overkill here? Revenge against the patriarchy? Generalized resentment against the unsatisfactory nature of life?

Who knows?

What vile act did Smith perpetrate? Did it involve a cattle-prod? Farm animals? Dunno. The papers did report a definition of harassment once given by Claudia the Combat-Ready: "His hand lingers on your back. He touches you on your upper arm and you can't tell if he's a touchy-feely person. All you know is that he gives you the creeps."

The horror.

Me, I'm trying to figure out the whole concept of sensitivity in generals. Generals are supposed to be warriors. I read that in a book somewhere. Here we have one coming unglued, positively delaminating, over something that middle-school girls handle every day.

I'm trying to picture a generalette at war. It's not easy. Historically women have been not warriors, but booty. (Why do you think all those guys with the swords and shields wanted to break into the city? Not to steal the crockery.) But I'm trying to be modern.

It's not going well.

Let us say that Pyong Yang decides to acquire Seoul. Massed artillery cuts loose in January. Wind howls along those bleak Korean valleys with paddies frozen to steel. Bullets whine, wounded scream, arms and legs fly through the air like migrating birds. Remorseless North Korean infantry run around with those pointy things on their rifles.

And here comes General Kennedy charging across the landscape, yelling, "*Squeeeeeeeeeeeeeeeeaaaaaaaaaaaak!* Don't *touch* me!"

I guess that's how most armies do it. Reckon?

What's really neat, though, is the response of the military leadership to this comic opera. The sensible thing here would be to say, "Larry, dammit man, how stupid can you get? Try a singles bar. Claudia, get a life. Now go away." End of problem.

But no. Our boss warriors are, characteristically, on their knees. When they retire, maybe they can make a living doing floors. A gal general says she was fondled and the entire military leadership wriggles and squirms like apologetic puppies who have wet the rug.

Lemme tell you why it happens.

The real power in the Pentagon is not the Joint Chiefs of Staff. They are just window dressing, suitable for swelling a uniform, or looking growly on occasions of state, or telling some hopeless sod of a president what he wants to hear.

The real power is something called DACOWITS. This is not an upper-case Polish mathematician, but rather the Defense Advisory Commission on Women in the Services. The Dacowitches are politically appointed civilian feminists, dedicated to demilitarizing the services.

They want to teach Marines to talk about their feelings. They are supported by What's-his-Porkrind in the White House, and the gender-loon machinery in congress. They run the Pentagon like dominatrixes in a Victorian bordello.

Think I'm kidding? Ask someone who works in the building.

They get what they want. What they want is not readiness for combat, about which they know little and care less. When I was covering the services a few years back, the Dacos had the military grasp of little fuzzy ducks. But nobody dares tell them to buzz off. Nobody. That's the end of the career.

You might ask why. Would Churchill, you might wonder, or Ike, or JEB Stuart, or any man at all, put up with this stuff from ill-tempered powderpuffs who think push-ups are bras? Would even the doorman at a unisex barbershop be so submissive?

After careful thought, I believe that there is only one reasonable conclusion:

The Joint Chiefs of Staff are transvestites.

You read it here first. JCS stands for Jasmine, Cygne, and Sue. Yep. In the Five-Sided Wind Box, it's Susan B. Anthony all the way. Only really it's Anthony B. Susan.

OK, OK. I don't really know that. I haven't asked them, and they haven't told. But I can't see any other explanation. They know perfectly well what the weird plague of countercultural enthusiasm is doing to the military. The public doesn't know, but the generals know.

They know that their men hold them in contempt, that guys are bailing out, pilots going to the airlines, recruiting becoming difficult. And they know it isn't the economy. It's the endless sensitivity training, and gay-appreciation, and unmarried women calving like moose in May, and Claudia, with her horror of creepy fingers on her back.

If the JCS were men, they wouldn't stand for it. So they must not be.

Which leaves crossdressers. It all fits. I figure they've got tu-tus in their closets, and the most darling feather boas.

Jasmine, Cygne, and Sue.

2

Manners. Suaveness. Deboneur-tude.

Let me tell you about aplomb. I don't mean watery New-Age aplomb, suitable for a fern bar. I mean the real article, forty-weight, that you could lube a diesel with.

This was in the early eighties. I was still a staff writer on *Soldier of Fortune* magazine. This was years before Craig, the staff artist, killed himself riding drunk on his motorcycle somewhere outside Boulder. He died, everyone said, as he would have wanted. Horribly.

In those days Craig and I hung out for a while in the Berkeley Bar in a bad section of Denver. Craig was a big, baby-faced street fighter out of Chicago with a Special Forces past and a mean streak. He mostly drew skulls. He also liked the Brandenburg concertos, and used to listen to them at his easel with headphones built into a World War II leather flying helmet.

The Berk was the home pit for the Sons of Silence, a bad biker club. If you haven't been in dives like this, don't start now. They swarm with huge bearded bozos with tattooed eyeballs and missing teeth and slow ominous grins and the IQ of a camshaft. You get the impression that they are evolving, but just not as fast as the rest of us. They'll hurt you. Either they like you or you're jelly. They don't worry about consequences. They can't remember them.

The Berk had Formica wood tables and smelled like a weight room. Rows of bottles waited patiently, but not for long, behind the counter, and corpulent biker babes lolled about like stranded elephant seals. No one else did. When you have a biker clientele, you don't have any other kind of clientele. Craig and I were guests. I had sold Bob Brown, the editor of *Soldier of Fortune*, on a story about the warm patriotic urges of the Sons, who didn't have any. The Sons were charmed. They might get on the cover. They knew they would never get closer to significance.

It was cold enough to freeze the personals off an iron dog and dirty snow gleamed yellow under the streetlights. We showed up in Craig's pickup truck, wearing our credentials: cammies, antisocial T-shirts ("Happiness Is A Confirmed Kill") and jump boots. A Tribal Meeting followed, heap big powwow, talk'em. Craig and I sat in a booth with Torque, the honcho, and a brain-fried guy called Lurch, and Mountain Jerry, who was a pretty Tarzan replica with long golden hair like Rapunzel and gold-flecked eyes that spoke of psychopathy and bone fractures. He sort of looked through you.

"We don't like the press," Torque said. So what? Nobody did. I didn't. Torque had a face like a gorilla's armpit. "You can do your story. *SOF*'s a righteous mag. Righteous." I guess it was a recommendation. Like having Carlo Gambino say that you were a Really Good Person.

"We do what we can," Craig said.

Lurch just stared at his beer with his mouth hanging open. He didn't actually drool, probably because he couldn't remember how. I figured he had smoked too much brass polish or sniffed some bad glue.

During this prayer meeting, Lurch had An Idea. You could tell it was bubbling up inside him. His jaw closed slightly and a crazed focus came into his eyes. He was going to say something, as soon as he figured out what. His head came up. Yes, an idea. He almost had it.

And then it left him. He collapsed with a soughing sound, like a punctured tire. Gone. A Real Idea, probably the unified field theory. And it got away. He stared sorrowfully at his beer. Eeyore of the Bikers.

We went back to the tribal thing.

Manners, though. This is about grace, elegance, and aplomb. Yeah.

Later we were boozing at the bar, doing what women call male bonding. It means talking to each other. I was chatting with Mountain Jerry. Craig was talking to some guy farther down the bar and drinking peppermint schnapps. Which was amazing on two counts. First, that the Berk had such an effeminate candy-ass yuppie-swine liqueur. Second, that Craig would drink it in a biker bar. It was grounds for execution.

Thing was, Craig was scary. He'd cripple you. You sensed he was ready to rock-and-roll, and you really didn't want to rumble with him. Some guys you leave alone. The Sons could smell it.

About then one of the biker babes got into it with the barmaid. I don't know what the raison de guerre was. The challenger was a gas-station Brunhilde like a sack of potatoes, except potatoes have better skin. Shrieking ensued. Barmaids in motorcycle hangouts do not back down. You could tell this one wasn't a Latin professor at Bryn Mawr. She screamed obscenities in a florid cloacal gush. The potato sack gave as good as she got.

The bikers ignored them and kept drinking. Jerry and I were discussing social encounters in rural bars in West Virginia, where we both came from. The chief instrument of intercourse in those regions was the pool cue. It was simple and direct and provided the hospitals with a brisk business.

Over Mountain Jerry's shoulder I saw the challenger's arm flash forward. She was throwing a bottle at the barmaid. Either her aim was bad or the barmaid ducked. Bottles shattered behind the bar and the mirror pretty much exploded. Slivers rained down on me, but missed my drink.

Mountain Jerry never flickered. He grinned his slow mean golden grin and said, "Git it on." And kept on talking. He was amused.

The bar top glittered with glass fragments. The barmaid was about to leap over the bar to do battle with Spud Sack. Screaming continued. Nobody paid the slightest attention. Down the bar I saw Craig absently, without looking, pull a sizable sliver of glass from his schnapps, without interrupting his sentence. He dipped a finger to see whether more shards awaited. No. All was well. He lifted the glass and drank.

That's aplomb.

3

A Codpiece For Bill

Tell you how we're going end the mess in Kosovo. We're going to buy Bill Clinton a codpiece.

I figure the whole thing is a manhood ritual. Have you seen those nature movies about swamp birds? You know: the male bird sticks his neck in the air like he thought it was a periscope and pumps his head up and down and gurgles weirdly and flaps and skitters across the water like an epileptic fit with feathers, and the female bird, who doesn't know any better, thinks, "*Oh, baby.*" That's what Clinton is doing in Kosovo. Waggling his virility.

A codpiece would do just as well, and be lots cheaper. I figure something in black leather, with a Harley logo.

Most wars are started by short, funny-looking men with weak egos. Napoleon, Mussolini, Hitler, Alexander the Great, Lenin, Trotsky—a congeries of pipsqueaks. Now, Bill isn't funny-looking, being cornpone handsome and reasonably presentable, but everyone knows he hid out during his generation's war, as shamelessly as Dan Quayle and Ron Reagan. (The difference between Clinton and Reagan is that...umm...er...heh...hmmm.) Anyway, Bill is always getting ragged about wussing out.

It galls him. Guys who went to war can affect trauma manfully borne, bear up under terrible memories they don't have, and work on their thousand-yard stares, even though most of them were in mess-kit repair battalions. Not Clinton. Bill didn't go. He stands to be remembered chiefly for mendacity and diddling fat girls. The military sneers at him. He's kind of pasty. You can't help feeling that if he stood in front of the tofu department at Safeway, he might end up in someone's cart.

He needs to bomb someone. It's remedial Quang Tri.

Why the Serbians? They probably deserved bombing, but most people do. Why them? Why not some other miscreants? What earthly reason do we have for such a thing?

The national interest? I did some research on Kosovo—checked atlases, pored over maps, studied GPS coordinates and history books, did latitudes and longitudes. I found out something fascinating: *Kosovo is in Europe.* Judging by Clinton's enthusiasm, I had figured it must be in Arkansas, maybe in the suburbs of Little Rock.

Now, it seems to me that if Kosovo is in Europe, it's Europe's problem. Near I as can tell, the United States is in no heart-stopping danger of invasion by Serbians. I have carefully counted all of Serbia's strategic missiles, carrier battle groups, fighter aircraft, and motorized armies, and the grand total would fit nicely into the IQ of a network anchorman. As a matter of cold-eyed military analysis, a couple of elderly senators from Mississippi with bird guns could defend us against Serbia.

So why are we over there? Europe is a remarkably useless place and, politically speaking, belongs in diapers. All it does is make trouble. Half of it invades the other half, which then comes squalling to us like a three-year-old to Mommy and wants us to save it from itself. Serbs are worse trouble. We got into World War I because a Serbian loon shot that archduke. It would have been cheaper to buy them another archduke, but no. We had to go save Europe.

It doesn't make sense. Kosovo isn't our problem. We're there, I tell you, so Clinton can work on his feral aura. He wants to be like James Dean, Elvis, and Marlon Brando. He'd have better luck trying to be a shorthaired poodle, but never mind.

A codpiece would be better all around. We would want a large one, of course, to better make the point. Throw in a raffish tattoo on the arm (I'm partial to "This End Up," though I suppose "Death Before Dishonor" or "Born to Die Hard" would better convey the presidential lethality), and everybody would know he was *one...ba-a-ad...dude.* (Or a dweeb with a codpiece, but I'm trying to be upbeat.)

Don't underestimate codpieces. They can be more than fashion statements. If it had a zipper the president could keep in it such utensils as might be convenient in his hobbies—mouthwash, ScotchGuard, maybe a panatela. There could be a pocket for car keys. Perhaps a radio transmitter so the Secret Service could keep track of him, though the antenna might be an embarrassment.

The more I think about it, the better the idea seems. We might include a smoke-generator in case a third-world mob assaulted him. Even if the smoke didn't hide him, astonishment at its source alone would paralyze the hardiest mob. How about a packet of shark repellant in case he fell out of a helicopter? A compartment for sandwiches? Kind of like a purse for guys.

If that didn't stop Bill's military lunging about, we could get him a sword.

4

The Underclass

We do not speak of the black underclass. We need to begin.

For over five years now I have gone as a reporter with the police, into the cities and the suburbs, into Washington, Chicago, Los Angeles, Denver. I have visited prisons and jails, spent night shifts in the precincts where whites don't go. What I have seen of the vast festering hordes of the black forgotten is grim. White America doesn't grasp the magnitude of the underclass, its isolation, its hopelessness, its resistance to change. Or its anger.

Go into the sprawling necrotic wastelands of the urban conglomerations. As you cross the racial divide, the world turns black, English changes, people walk differently, body language alters. In eight hours in a police car you will never see a white face. Broken windows in abandoned buildings gape at the night, home to crackheads and derelicts. Lean young men gaze at police cars with blank hostile eyes.

Go, say, to South Chicago (actually, don't: you wouldn't last an hour) where the city warehouses unwanted blacks in huge high-rise projects, ugly megaliths erupting from bleak concrete, with their own police stations and terrible schools with dropout rates of seventy-five percent. Go into homes where in mid-afternoon a half-dozen men sit listlessly before the television, along streets where they sit for hours on stoops, doing nothing. There is nothing for them to do.

The isolation of these people from the surrounding country, from anything at all except the ghetto, is near absolute. For months on end black kids here never see a white face, except on television. Nothing connects them emotionally with the greater society. They have nothing in common with the European heritage of the United States, know little of it. These are people who don't know that the English Channel separates England and France, can't tell you within a hundred years when World War I was fought or who fought it, aren't aware of ever having heard of the Bill of Rights, have never read an entire book. About anything. Ever.

If you think I'm exaggerating, think again.

Not European, not American in the usual sense, neither are they African, though they sometimes grasp at African-ness so as to have a sense of belonging. They can't name two African countries, or find Africa on an outline map of the world. They aren't African. They are urban blacks of the deep city.

The underclass does not change. Nice suburban whites hear of the growth of the black middle class, marvel at the sight of black men dating blonde Anglo women, and think that the country moves toward interracial amity. Don't kid yourself. The center of gravity of black America is the ghetto. It doesn't shrink as some few of its residents pull themselves into the middle class and leave. Maybe it grows.

The underclass is so large, so insular, that the slight mixing around the edges can't diminish it. The ghetto is self-sustaining, a world unto itself. The United States has become a first-world European nation with Kenya distributed throughout it.

The cultural gap probably widens. White America races ahead, measuring its advance in megahertz and the colonization of cyberspace. The black middle class largely keeps pace. The underclass barely knows how to read. Welfare and television, our latter-day bread and circuses, keep the lid on. Explosions come, as witness the riots in Los Angeles, but they are few. In the short term they will likely remain few. We have learned how to sedate the ghetto.

We have not learned what to do about it.

The newspapers, seldom much aware of what happens around them, speak of prejudice and oppression. Blacks of the huge, rotting, unseen downtown do not suffer from discrimination or oppression. Rather they suffer from abandonment. Nobody needs or wants them. They cannot do anything that anyone wants done. Whites feed them, talk solicitously when they remember the city at all, and live elsewhere.

If whites can do nothing about the underclass, neither can the underclass. The culture of the ghetto resists change. Many whites think of black culture as meaning an embarrassing incompetence that needs only to learn the superiority of advanced European ways. No. Black culture exists. It is rich, warm, vibrant, classy, pungent, and it is the same from Philadelphia to San Diego. Blacks like it. They don't want to be white. They don't speak the bastardized English of downtown because they couldn't learn to say, "He is" instead of, "He be." Even to white eyes there is a certain gelded quality to a black executive speaking precise white English.

We have become two nations sharing a country.

Economics works against change. No academic urge is found in the ghetto, no entrepreneurial vitality, none of the traits that make for success in a techno-industrial society. The ghetto is permanent. Hispanics seem to be pulling themselves up the ladder in the long tradition of America's immigrants, Asians do it readily, but the forgotten blacks of the ghetto don't.

What now? Do we expect things to remain stable forever? Have we, as seems to be the case, decided that no solution exists, and therefore we might as well ignore the problem? I think so. The enthusiasms of the era of civil rights have waned. Whites have moved on to other things. My circle of acquaintances, sophisticated in the ways of politics, seldom mention the chasm and, when they do, it is to concede its utter intractability.

People don't say it, not often, but they think it: There is nothing we can do. Meanwhile hatred gathers in the urban blasted heath. The riots of Los Angeles could have happened anywhere. The people of the ghetto believe that whites are the cause of their misery, and they are, just under the surface, very angry. One day this is going to bite us.

5

A Revisionist View Of Bars

We're not supposed to go to bars any more. I hear it from substance-abuse do-gooders, self-absorbed as all Calvinists, who pop Prozac and lithium and Xanax and Zoloft and worry dreadfully about beer. Sometimes I gotta wonder about do-gooders, Maybe there's such as thing as doing too much good.

Stray thought: When did beer get to be a substance?

Funny: As I look back with satisfaction over a thus-far misspent life, I notice that a lot of my best memories happened in bars. Like maybe in some country-and-western honkytonk up a holler in Tennessee, with a big neon Budweiser sign glowing red in the window and a friendly bar maid with a sunny smile and no shortage of beer.

Or maybe in Linda's Surprise Club in Bangkok with old friends from other and stranger times, flirting with the girls and telling war stories about the odd things that happen to people who have lives (which I don't think includes do-gooders), with mama-san bringing big brown bottles of Singha. Or maybe in the press bar in Nairobi, with some guy from Reuters telling about walking into what he thought was a traditional dance but turned out it was machete fight and....

You know the kind of story you hear in bars: "So there we were in Snake Alley in Taipei, and O'Toole, big doofus Irishman with this parrot on his shoulder that he bought somewhere, well, O'Toole picks up some hooker with three thumbs—yeah, it was a mutation or something, and...."

But it's always a *bar*, or other venue equipped with brew. Somehow I don't think it's a coincidence. Pubs and dram houses are where folks laugh and remember the wild places and crazy times and generally celebrate the occasional splendor of this otherwise sorry existence.

Am I wrong?

Usually there's music. Maybe a purple jukebox wailing country tunes about fast cars and faster women. Or a blues outfit telling of hard times and knife fights in a thousand gin mills in Depression-era Chicago. Or a bar band picking and planking songs about bad divorces and sorry paychecks and yore cheatin' heart and how Mama got run over by a big old train. Bar music is the stuff of real life.

Yeah, and couples two-stepping and guys in cowboy hats swapping lies with their foot on the brass rail along the bar and usually there's smoke in the air. Air doesn't smell right without smoke. The women look like women and the men look like men in bars. I mean real bars, not yuppy fernatariums where the little sogs talk about their feelings. In a real bar, usually you got a couple of guys shooting pool with their girlfriends over by the juke box, with cigarettes hanging from the corner of their mouth. That's how it ought to be.

Bar bands mostly play funky down-home stuff: blues, C&W, rock. I claim they represent a good slice of what's worth keeping in American culture. Sure, I listened to classical when I was a kid. It was what the hippopotamus danced to on that Disney show. And I admit it: Beethoven was pretty good for a deaf guy. But that's like saying ol' Charlie was a pretty good running back, except he was blind and didn't have any legs. I figure the Europeans listened to Beethoven because Little Richard hadn't been invented.

Now, some people do abuse beer. They turn into drunks and messes and run over people in their cars. I guess they shouldn't. If you're stupid enough, you can overdo anything. You can eat till you look like an unused breast implant with legs and have a heart attack every ten minutes, or max out six credit cards at eighteen percent, or put too much torque on a head bolt. That doesn't mean you should stop eating, or not use bolts and keep your cylinder head balanced on the engine block, and drive real slow over bumps so it doesn't fall off.

Beer has its virtue. Always has, always will. Fact is, this world doesn't amount to much unless you give it a little amplification sometimes. You have to encourage it. The dross is there, but you can find bits of gold sometimes. Take good companions, a pitcher of malt lubricant, add a good blues mouth-harp that sounds like broken hearts or a cat fight, depending, or a country band singing philosophy like, "Life's an Infomercial (Actual Results May Vary.)" Toss in a slab of ribs and some really raunchy barbecued beans and a plate of fritters.

Now, that's *meaning*. We don't get a whole lot of it.

Tell you what. If you want to sit around your living room and drink designer water with painfully nice people who avoid second-hand smoke and dress carefully and have the personality of potted plants, it's your business. You'll probably live longer, though I'm not sure why you'd want to.

But I hear The Towering Bouffants, one of my favorite bar bands, are playing old rock at Whitey's tonight, and I'm gonna go listen. And heist a brew or two and eat a great big greasy bacon cheeseburger with ketchup running out of it.

And when my time comes to leave this curious world, and PCS out of wherever we are, I hope I go to the great C&W dive in the sky, where they have ribs with really good sauce and maybe a little garlic, and an unending tap of Bud and people laughing, and a good-pickin' band and the gals twirling and two-stepping around the floor till a dawn that never comes.

6

Against Marriage

Mostly when I hear one of these radical feminist ladies squawking and clucking about whatever is disturbing her system at the moment, I don't listen a whole lot, because most of them have the insight of flatworms and run on pure bile. But I have to agree with them about marriage. It's a bad idea.

For a guy, I mean. If you're a woman, listen to the feminists. They'll tell you why marriage is a bad idea for women: Men are rapists. All of us. We batter women like cannibal tempura chefs. We don't have feelings. We're no damn good.

Take their advice. Stay away from us.

But let me tell you why marriage is bad for guys. If you're a young fellow thinking about tying the awful knot, read this carefully.

Guys marry for bad reasons. When it comes to women, we have less judgment than bugs in a moonshine bottle. Guys marry charm. They marry a sweet smile, a perky toss of the chin. They marry clear skin and bright eyes, soft lips, warm hands. They marry curves in a pretty print dress and silken hair that smells like warm milk and new-mown grass. (Maybe that's straining the language. Steinbeck or somebody said it.) Men marry necking on back roads, with crickets creaking in the woods and warm breezes and Sally is just so unspeakably wonderful they can't do without her.

Men marry illusion. Sally marries a pre-med.

We males have an infinite capacity for deluding ourselves. The charm of women doesn't last, any more than flowers in a mountain meadow. A requirement for a marriage license should be that the guy spend fifteen minutes thinking of Sally as twenty pounds heavier with crow's feet and PMS and no further incentive to control it.

In five years she won't want to party. Little Richard will give way to easy listening. In a decade she won't even slightly resemble the lissome damsel he married. She won't like his friends unless they're boring. The fun and excitement will fade and life will be just life.

Charm has a short shelf-life. A fellow should ask himself: Is her mind such that he wants to spend forty years talking to her?

Maybe so. Some women are great that way. One was reported in San Francisco a few years ago, and I know of one in Canada. (Actually a fair number of gals are seriously bright, and lots are reasonably interesting. But Willy Bill probably won't marry one. Anyway, ask yourself the question.)

However, the overarching aspect of marriage, the one that ought to be part of the dictionary definition, is that Sally will get the children. She'll get the house too, but the world is full of houses. The kids are the killer.

Women have a mysterious power to fog men's minds. I hear Willy Bill saying, "Divorce? Impossible. Sally's adorable. Even if it happened, we'd still be friends." There was a case of this reported too. In central China, before Confucius. Scholars debate its authenticity.

Willy Bill very likely will get divorced, which will very likely be Sally's idea, and she will get the kids with virtual certainty. Further (and he won't believe it in the full flood of hormonal misjudgment) she will in all likelihood use them against him. Even if not, she'll remarry and move to the other end of the country, and he will be lucky if he sees the kids a week at Christmas. Willy Bill now faces fifteen years of child support for children he will barely know. At best Sally will be heartless about it, at worst vengeful. The courts will support her every step of the way.

If you think this doesn't happen, regularly, think again. Think several times.

The way to avoid the morass is simply not to marry. Thanks to the Sexual Revolution, guys don't have to. Find one you like and live with her. If you get along, keep on living together. Maybe you will have a long, happy life together. It happens.

However, most women give the marry-me-or-leave ultimatum in about two years max, which means that you'll have to find another. This is unpleasant, but then the variety is nice. Serial monagamy isn't too bad. (I personally prefer parallel monogamy, but it isn't real practical.)

Once you tie the knot, your house is toast. But the for-keeps break-point, the one that really hurts, is children. Dead serious, guys, watch this one. Here, Sally holds all the high cards. I talk to a lot of men who are going crazy because the ex just remarried and went to Oregon with the kids.

They do this. All the time.

Remember that after the divorce, Sally is going to hate you. The divorce will have been your fault. You will have failed her in every way. You won't have met her expectations. That's the opening hand.

She will want to remarry. Fine. If you're crazy, maybe you will want to remarry. How much do you think she's going to want you around, after she has re-daddied your children? Is she going to tell New Daddy he can't take that promotion in Oregon because of your rights to see your kids?

As a rule, she won't concede that you have a right to see your sprats, or that they have any stake in seeing their father. Her rationale will be the passive-aggressive formulation, "Well, he's so insensitive I just can't believe he really wants to see them, blah blah blah."

This is Sally, remember, with the perky smile and soft lips.

Don't do it, guys. At least, don't do it unless you have a bomb-proof pre-nup saying that when the divorce comes, either party who leaves the region has to leave the kids with the other. And the courts today are disregarding pre-nups.

It's a hell of a way to begin a marriage. But do it. Do it because you can count on one thing: The courts will be absolutely on her side.

Better yet, if you want kids, go to Asia and marry. The women are feminine (consult your dictionary), beautiful, agreeable (consult your dictionary), and don't have cellulite.

Don't marry, guys. Stay single. The feminists are right on this one. And when you get married anyway and lose the house and kids, remember that weird columnist who said it would happen, and he was right.

7

"DOA in Progress"

Police are not like you and me—not, anyway, after a year on the job. Urban cops live in what amounts to a parallel world, in the city we all know but somehow a different city, sordid, hidden from the respectable middle-class, dangerous, peopled by creatures who seem barely human. It changes them.

Cops see the grotesque, the inexplicable, the scarcely credible. On a hot night in August we found the guy in the bushes near National Airport who two weeks earlier, having lost his girlfriend, had put a bullet through his head. The stench was awful, a rancid sick reek. The guy's face was sliding off his skull and his spine was a white rod visible through his chest. Some of the cops were breathing through their mouths to avoid gagging.

"Think CPR would help?" someone asked.

They hide in black humor. It seems callous, uncaring. It isn't. It's a shield.

Months later one of them told me, "The only way I kept from puking was, no way was I going to do it in front of a reporter."

A cop sees the worst of humanity, and the best of humanity at their worst. Even good people seem repulsive to cops: the banker, stopped for speeding, huffing and puffing about how important he is; the woman hiking her skirt and flirting; others lying, lying, lying. A cop never goes where good things are happening. A woman doesn't call 911 to say that she passed her mammogram, her husband hasn't had a drink in five years, and the kids aced their SATs. Instead a cop goes into homes on domestic calls and finds couples glaring at each other in hatred while the kids cry in the corner because mommy and daddy are fighting.

So much of the cop world is ugly. You answer a check-on-welfare call and find an old woman passed out on the floor with her husband wandering around bumping off walls. Literally bouncing: Dazed shuffle, bump, startle, turn and shuffle till he hits another wall. Maybe dementia, maybe Alzheimer's.

Or maybe he knows he's losing his wife of fifty years, and just turned his head off.

Fire-department med-techs arrive. The woman's blood pressure is 310/180. You could rupture a truck tire with that. They carry her out. "Pressure's rising," says the paramedic in the ambulance.

DOA in progress. She's not going to last. The radio says a gang fight is developing, so off you go.

This happened.

How does a cop handle it? With difficulty. It never stops. You go to the hospital to interview the rape victim, age fifteen, because you need a description. She's sobbing hysterically, half out of her mind. They're sedating her. The dirtball really knocked her around: bad facial bruises, split lip. Every cell in your body wants to find the guy and beat him until he doesn't have an intact bone. Brutality has its appeal. It really does.

You have to turn off, not get involved.

Americans are insulated from death. Cops see a lot of it. So do others in the street trades: shock-trauma surgeons, ambulance crews, fire departments, ER nurses. It isn't pretty movie-death. It's the grandmother who stroked out in the bathtub three days ago, and the flies beat you to her. It's the teenage Cambodian gangbanger—shot in the head, still breathing, with brain tissue swelling out of the hole like obscene lips.

DOA in progress.

You turn off. You have to. I remember a wreck at a brightly-lit intersection in suburban Maryland. Some idiot had been speeding real bad and flipped his pickup. He didn't roll it—the sides weren't scratched. The truck went airborne and landed on the top. The driver came out the windshield.

There were a dozen squad cars and several ambulances. The street was blocked off with police tape. The bar lights on the squads flashed *red-blue red-blue*. The med-techs, two guys and a gal, were working on what was left of the driver.

DOA in progress. Red mush was coming out of his mouth, and they were trying to intubate him and pump his chest at the same time. Waste of time. They knew it. You gotta try. It's one of the rules.

Another med-tech, a woman, knew the cop I was with. She smiled and called to him. I remember the question: "Bob! How's your wife?" They chatted. Ten feet behind her the rest of her team were losing this guy. *Pump, pump, pump.* The woman in the group dived into a medical bag for something that wouldn't work either with the tight, controlled speed they get when everything is on the line. And we were laughing and telling stories.

Self-preservation. Do the job, but don't get involved.

The kids are the worst. Old people are going to die anyway. Adults— well, they're all grown up. But the ones that really get to cops are kids deliberately hurt. Lots of cops refuse to work in kid-abuse units because, they say, "I'm afraid I'd kill somebody."

There a cop learns things he doesn't want to know. He learns, for example, that if you splash boiling water on a three-year-old girl, you get pink swollen splotches. If you hold her hands under boiling water, you get puffy pink lines of demarcation between burned and unburned flesh. These are called "immersion cuffs."

It happens. Usually the mother does it. Men commit more crime, and the violent crime, but women do more of the child abuse. Their dirtball boyfriends do a lot of it too.

You don't have to ride long in a squad car before you recognize that "scum" is a real social category. It isn't a politically correct category. You can't speak of scum in newspapers. They exist.

For example, the derelicts who urinate on the sidewalk in plain sight of children, or break into an unoccupied house and live there, using one room as a toilet. The child-molesters. And worse: The couple (it happened, right here in the nation's capital) who kept their small daughter tied up for months, causing rope-burn on unhealed rope-burns, tortured her, fed her so little that she was thirty-nine pounds underweight, and then stuffed her in a closet, tied in a jacket with the hood turned around backward. She suffocated.

Scum. They're a cops world.

8

Trouble at the Daily Planet

I figure we'll take newspaper editors, and shove'm into a woodchipper, and make mulch. They look absorbent. Thing is, if you planted corn in shredded editors, it would probably grow sideways, because it wouldn't know which way was up.

Now I gotta figure out whether there's a market for sideways corn. Journalism is harder than it looks.

Anyway, editors. A passel of the rascals got together a while back, at some trade show, to wonder why circulation was falling, and people thought journalists were no-account scoundrels, lower than possums and education theorists. They all wondered together in unison and in three-part harmony, and came away empty.

They didn't know why people are sick of newspapers.

I could give them an idea. Start with the calculated mendacity of reporters. The truth ain't in'em. Journalism is a kitchen I work in, so I see what goes into the soup.

For instance, remember all the stories about how the military was buying toilet seats for $600, and $17 bolts? Neither happened. I checked a lot of those tales as a military writer. They generally amounted to fabrication. The Pentagon has all manner of ways to waste money, but bolts and toilet seats aren't among them.

I'll tell you how the lying is done. The details and numbers won't be right, or even real close, because I'm remembering from years back, but you'll get the point.

The Navy ages ago bought an airplane called the A-3 that looked like a black-eyed pea with wings and was supposed to chunk atomic bombs on the Russians. (You've heard the Navy's recipe for Chicken Kiev? Heat the city to four million degrees and throw in a chicken.) The A-3 had a design life of twenty years. Crashing daily on a carrier ages a plane. (The Navy calls it "landing." I've seen it done, and I say it's crashing.)

Anyway, the A-3, like most airplanes, had a number of nonstandard parts. One was an odd bolt for the nose gear. The Navy bought enough bolts for twenty years. Then Congress decided to extend the service life of the A-3 by several years. The Navy, now about out of bolts, needed a few more.

There are two ways to get a few bolts. One is to go to a bulk-bolt shop and order 10,000. They'll cost a buck each, for a total bill of $10,000. You'll use ten and toss the rest overboard. The other way is to get a machine shop to make ten bolts by hand. This is expensive. Those ten bolts might cost $170.

"NAVY BUYS SEVENTEEN-DOLLAR BOLTS!"

That's how the game is played. I could give many examples of no interest today, including the $600 toilet seat.

Is it technically lying? Maybe not.

But is it really? Yep.

Does it happen all the time?

You bet it does. And people figure out that they're being lied to.

Now, you might wonder why the media engage in crafted prevarication. As best I can tell, it begins with their being predominantly a group that has little in common with most, or certainly a very large part, of America. That doesn't make them liars. But it's a step.

If you checked the newsroom of the *Washington Post*, I suspect you would find that the inmates mostly lived in pricey neighborhoods, had degrees from Princeton, drank white wine, and ate salads made from strangely named vegetables. Most of them, I'll bet you, have never baited a hook, changed their oil, or made a raft out of orange crates and old inner tubes.

Nor (I'm continuing to bet) have they ever held a gun, much less fired one, and would regard doing so as highly exotic and probably fascistic. Zero of them would have served in the military. The men likely never got into a fight in high school. The women probably think that peeing in the woods constitutes either grave hardship or high adventure. Few have hitchhiked, boozed in a country bar, done shift work in a gas station, pulled crab pots, or played in a tire swing.

In short, they are privileged little snots. And have the attitudes to go with it. They don't like, among other things, the military, rural people, guns, the South, traditional morality, and Marlboro Man.

Now, here you have to understand the peculiar mental habitat that is journalism. Reporters, having power without responsibility, come to think they deserve it, and grow lordly. (I have one of those buttons you wear on a shirt that says, "Power Corrupts. Absolute Power Is Kind Of Neat." Exactly.)

The trade encourages you to be impressed with yourself. You can go almost anywhere, do almost anything, and everyone is afraid of what you might write. Directly or by implication, you get to tell people how they ought to think and live. It's heady stuff, especially for a minor intelligence with a ticket from J-school.

The clout is exhilarating. If you call the Pentagon and say, Hey, can I fly in an F-16 and do a low-level pop-and-drop bombing run, the Air Force will say, "Yessir, Mr. Reed, splendid idea, how intelligent of you to think of it! Shall we land it on your sidewalk? What kind of dressing do you want on your salad?"

Nobody at the Pentagon will ever tell a reporter, "No, you dismal flatworm, the bullet comes out the *other* end." They will assuredly think it.

In journalism, merit has nothing to do with the importance assigned to you. You don't need merit, and few have it. In fact, the worse you are, the more respect you get, because stupidity allied with unpredictability is just flat awesome.

Reporters forget this. They forget it easily because journalism is a performing art, and attracts egos that inflate as readily as airbags.

Soon you begin to believe that your business is not to inform, but to instruct. You know that you are right about...well, about everything, because everybody in the newsroom agrees with you. (Diversity in newspapering means that you have blacks who think exactly the same things you do, Hispanics who think exactly...)

The result is a kindergarten of privileged little snots, insular, arrogant, convinced of their superiority, thinking in lockstep, ignorant without knowing it, invincibly self-assured, who want to Make Things Better. They want to improve you. They want you to share their enlightenment, want to herd you in directions good for you. They are missionaries to the bushmen. You and me.

Mulch. It's the only answer.

9

Chuckie Manson, Thor, and The Ark

In the year of the Great Radioactive Goat-Curd Craze and Flood-That-Wasn't, Matamoscas was just another sleepy California town in the high desert near Barstow. The only feature of note anywhere near was a low mesa called Las Pulgas, about three miles out of town where the Ark was.

About a year before, a peyote-enhanced guru named Mahmud al Gravid, who looked like Charles Manson but probably wasn't, had descended on the town with his followers. Gravid had the deeply spiritual look that comes of minor brain damage and exposure to Los Angeles. His followers were scrofulous late-adolescents with love beads. Being teenagers, they thought the world had been invented yesterday and they were the only ones who knew anything about it, especially as regarded matters spiritual. They said they were in Matamoscas to find themselves.

It was a good place to look, because that was where they were.

Anyway, Gravid had received from on high a notification that a Great Flood would soon wash away the world, beginning for reasons not immediately obvious with Matamoscas. Gravid and his lemmings were to prepare by building an Ark on Las Pulgas, made of cubits. They weren't sure what cubits were, but figured they would find them in the desert. It didn't hold together Biblically. They didn't know it, so it didn't matter.

They built an Ark that would have foundered in a heavy dew and awaited the flood.

For California the idea wasn't peculiar enough to stand out from the background, so the locals mostly drove around in pickups and drank beer in the town's only bar and ignored the seers out on the mountain. Given the way the Coast was pulling down the aquifers, they weren't really worried about a flood. They would have started one if they had known how.

Then Otto Swedenborg, a huge square-shouldered Scowegian meatball out of Minnesota, roared in on a Harley hog with a little trailer in tow. He looked like Thor and had eyes the color of swimming pools. The trailer contained pickle jars of Radioactive Goat-Curd, he said, which would cure anything, and make one's aura resonate with the inner force of being. He had discovered it while raising goats in land containing uranium ore. Ten bucks.

The locals needed radioactive goat curd like they needed a third elbow, so they sent him to the mountain. They figured nuts rolled uphill, and there was no other hill around.

Gravid apparently saw Swedenborg as a threat to his position as alpha-nutcase. In the ensuing tension, one of the followers said the hell with it and went back to L.A., where her father was big with CBS. A camera truck duly showed up at Las Pulgas. The whole kit and caboodle were on national television that night, auras resonating. Swedenborg got thirty seconds to expound the virtues of his goatish pudding.

The results were astonishing and unexpected. Goat curd took hold of the Californian imagination. First a trickle and then a flood of seekers of enlightenment began to show up in Matamoscas. They were a cross-section of the state: vegetarians, Hare Krishnas, sun-worshipers, fruit-juice drinkers, Ethical Culturists, and a residue of the Orgone Box movement. There were coked-up aspiring movie-stars who had believed the desert was a large beach, and Valley Girls who thought the whole idea was groovy to the max. Matamoscas was overrun.

Having manufactured the event, television also covered it. A reporter asked a slack-jawed blonde beachboy, who seemed to have the IQ of a shinplaster, how he felt about the new spiritual order.

"Well, I, like, you know, I think it's really true."

"What's true?"

"I'm not sure yet."

Swedenborg did land-office business in radioactive goat-curd. In fact, he ran out the first day, and resorted to selling jars of mayonnaise from the local grocery, after taking the labels off. The price went up like taxes in a Democratic administration. When asked how to use the curd to greatest inner advantage, he said to let it age for a week, and then rub it liberally over the entire body. The customer presumably ended up looking like a frankfurter in search of a roll.

There was talk of building a theme park in Matamoscas based on goat curd, as well as a hotel with a golf course, and a factory to turn out soy-based curd-substitute. Several hotel chains expressed interest. Investors were sought to buy a reactor. Swedenborg was offered a high position that didn't require that he be able to do anything. Matamoscas was On Its Way.

Then ABC, concerned about its slide in the ratings, reported that in the cliffs along Route 101-A, out of San Francisco, a rock formation had been found that was an unmistakable likeness of Che Guevara. It glowed in the dark and wept tears of proletarian solidarity, said a professor of psychiatry from Berkeley. He had discovered the likeness while processing his issues among the rocks with the help of some really dynamite mescaline. You could just feel the essence of Che trying to communicate some message of importance to all mankind.

Next morning, Matamoscas was empty. The spiritual freight train had moved on. Swedenborg left with his remaining jars of mayonnaise. Gravid and his followers vanished. The locals went back to driving around in pickups and drinking beer at the bar. The Ark is still there.

None of this happened. But it's all true.

10

The Rowboat As Nuclear Delivery System. Nukes in Plain Brown Wrappers.

I'm trying to understand Ballistic Missile Defense. It's slow going. Probably I need another cup of coffee.

Years ago, I did understand it, sort of. It used to be, the Russians were going to launch a totalitarian, rotten, inconsiderate world-domination attack, unexpectedly on a wet night, with ten gazillion nuclear missiles, give or take a dozen, and scramble our eggs most spectacular. So we needed to build a bunch of rockets to shoot down their rockets, which we could do for only several hundred bazillion dollars, plus a three-times overrun probably written into the contract. The Pentagram formed BMDO, the Ballistic Missile Defense Organization (Bam-dough to those who knew and loved it, because, *bam!*, it blew a lot of dough) to create jobs in Southern California.

Shoot down missiles, I mean.

OK. It made perfect sense.

Or at least it might have, except that for the same money we could have bought Russia, compacted it, and moved it to Nevada where we could watch it. Besides, I figure the Russian rocket forces would have sold out for two pairs of blue jeans each plus a twelve-dollar digital watch and a subscription to *Playboy*. It seemed to me we were doing things the hard way.

The federal government can't run a slum-clearance project. It was going to shoot down missiles? If even fifty of those suckers hit their targets, which is about what you would expect from three thousand Russian missiles, it wouldn't matter what the others did. If you vaporized the big American cities that make replacement parts for tractors, this country would shrivel like a moth in a bug-zapper. Complicated countries can't fight nuclear wars. It's just how things are.

And I could never see why the Russians would have wanted to attack. I knew, and they knew, that the Navy's missile subs would have turned Russia into one big glass-flat. Afterwards you could have tied fatback on your feet and skated from Kiev to Vladivostok. Russia barely worked the best day it ever saw. I couldn't see how being turned into radioactive glass would help much.

But then, I'm slow.

Ahh, but now, howsomever, we're going to build a little tiny Bam-dough to shoot down missiles from Rogue States. This means North Korea, Iran, and Iraq. These places want an ICBM to point at the US. It's to improve their self-esteem. North Korea is busily concocting missiles, including one unimposingly named, so help me, the No Dong. We guess they'll launch their one missile in a huff, or maybe by accident, and we'll shoot it down with micro-Bam-dough, *plink*. (You know how accidental launches are. There's a big red switch that says, "Fry Imperialist Rice," and you can stumble on a loose marble or something, and, Ooops…)

I don't get it. You don't need a missile to blow up Manhattan.

If you want to send a thousand bombs, you need a passel of missiles. To send one, you need a credit card and a shipping station. If I had a bomb or two, and wanted to blow up New York (which I might), I'd put it in a crate marked "Machine Tools" and send it to La Guardia by Air India. For really good precision, Fed-Ex would be better if you could get a bomb that fit their weight limits. A better-than-average third-world missile might hit the right continent. UPS will hand it to somebody in the right *room*. And their rates are good.

You don't even need that. Guys at DEA say that about 95% of the drugs that try to come into this country get in uncaught. How hard would it be to bring that nuclear bonbon ashore in a motorboat, put it in a '48 Ford flathead pickup truck, and drive it to Washington? Best I can tell, you could write "Cocaine" on it, and take it in a convertible, and nobody would notice.

The problem isn't countries. North Korea doesn't worry me. They've started talking to South Korea. They're going to discover money and food. It's gonna sap their will. They won't want to get in a nuclear war with the United States any more.

The real problem's more likely to be some sorry pack of free-lance losers with a bank account, a rowboat, and a highly perceptive inferiority complex. Not a country at all: Just scrofulous terrorists all riled up over some cause they don't understand. Someday, they might get a Bomb.

What I want to know is: What do we do when Chicago disappears? Ker-whoom? Who do we blow up in revenge? Everybody?

It's a problem. If Iraq nuked us, we'd turn the place into a geologic lava-lamp, and they know it. So they won't. But if the Red People's Liberation Jihad Army Hoopty-Squat Dirtbag Guevarist Fifth-of Some-Month Movement did it, well, we might catch a few of them. But so what? Hoopty-squat dirtbags are easy to replace. Assuming you want more of them.

We know how to get even with a country. We don't know how to get even with six congenitally furious goat-herds from an unsuccessful culture with too much sand.

Anyway, the thing about truck-nuking a city is that one time would be enough. All the other cities, or at least the obvious ones like Washington and New York, would empty overnight. If New York went, would *you* keep working on Capitol Hill? And of course every mayor in the country would be getting notes saying, "We blew up Chicago. Put a whole bunch of money in a locker in the bus station, or you're next." Most of them would be lying.

There would be no way to keep it from happening again. Not, anyway, without turning the country into a police state that would drive Joe Stalin into the ACLU.

What do you do when you know the bad guys had at least one bomb, because Chicago is having a warm winter and everybody downwind is mutating, and the spook agencies say the same loons have a couple more? Do you put radiation detectors on every road going into the big cities? Tap every phone and Hotmail account on earth? Eliminate private aviation? Put soldiers ten feet apart along the entire border, of which there's only a near-infinite amount? Stop letting freight come into the country?

Tell you what. I don't want ballistic-missile defense. Just give me a radiation suit and a ticket to Tierra del Fuego.

11

Prowess, Sort Of

The abyss is everywhere, the unknown chasm that lies beyond the world we think we understand. Especially in carburetors. The other day I went to the back yard to change the main jet on the carburetor that engages in respiration for my '67 Dodge. It is a simple device, having none of the incomprehensible swirls of anti-pollutional hoses that festoon modern machines like malign linguini.

Changing the jet is a simple matter of unscrewing one sorry little metal doughnut and replacing it with another. All you need is a screwdriver, long skinny fingers, four arms, and an ability to see through sheet metal.

Okay. I advanced on the old bucket with a box of tools and a *Soldier of Fortune* T-shirt: modern American manhood at its clear-eyed, technically adept finest. I scowled. I endeavored to look masterful. No office-serf like me can do anything practical without (a) a sense of wonder that it actually worked and (b) a giddy exultation at his prowess. Whenever I successfully repack the wheel bearings, I have an urge to put my foot on a log, beat my chest, and utter a long quavering shriek. Unfortunately the neighbors, jealous types, would send for a struggle buggy and a couple of big orderlies.

The hood went up nicely. Say "Ahhh." I am the equal of anybody in my mastery of hoods. The float bowl came off easily. Anything mechanical comes apart easily, often leaping spontaneously into more parts than you knew it had. The Second Law of Thermodynamics, which insists that the universe tends to disorder with devilish single-mindedness, was no doubt discovered by a physicist working on his carburetor.

The old jet came out easily. The new one screwed in simply…well, almost simply, if only my fingers would fit behind the float, but there was no serious problem. I'd just take a long screwdriver, hold the jet balanced with the tip, turn it slowly….

Actually, there was no great difficulty at all. I merely put my foot on the battery for balance, holding a small flashlight in my mouth to shine into the carburetor, held the float with one hand and guided the jet with the other. Easy. Unfortunately it didn't leave a hand to hold the screwdriver. The solution was really quite simple. All I had to do was….

After 45 minutes, my wife came out. She is by profession a harpsichordist and has the eye-hand coordination to disassemble a watch while bouncing on a trampoline. She does not, however, understand masterfulness. She tried to insert the jet a few times.

"This is ridiculous. Are you sure this is the right part?"

It was the wrong question to ask of embattled prowess.

My father came out to try. He had been skulking about, waiting for me to fail entirely so that he would be more impressive when he succeeded. He assumed a masterful expression and had at the vile device with the deft touch of a trained surgeon.

"Damn!"

"What?" I asked.

"I dropped it."

A principle of automotive mechanics is that all parts smaller than a tire look exactly like gravel. I put the patient jalopy in neutral and we pushed it back a yard to look beneath it. We got down on our knees and began peering at the driveway, trying to convey by a sort of panicked casualness that we were in command of the situation. Nothing. I began throwing gravel piece by piece into the woods on the theory that whatever remained would have to be the jet.

Judging by the sun, we had about three hours of daylight left.

Having found the thing at last, my father impaled it by its slot on an outsize screwdriver and began poking it at the carburetor like a dirk. He certainly looked masterful. I imagined him as a sort of latter-day D'Artagnan crossing swords with the enemies of the Crown, and leaving them with carburetor jets screwed into their breasts.

"Is it working?" I asked.

"Nothing to it. Used this trick for years, putting number-10 screws into junction boxes. Damn!"

We rolled the car back again and began searching for the jet. Five minutes later we did it again. My father looked down the driveway with a masterful expression that was beginning to be tinged with realism.

"I calculate we've got about 600 more feet of driveway," he said.

Automotive repair breaks into two phases—the first, in which the mechanic wants to fix the device, and the second, in which he wants to kill it. The difference between an obstacle and an enemy is about an hour and a half. Rage builds. It begins as a sort of interior itch accompanied by a desire to flex the large muscles. Then the fingers begin to curl uncontrollably. They are wondering what part of a carburetor might be the neck. Yet you still have to work delicately, precisely, or else call a mechanic. We tried.

"Damn!"

12

Modern Girls and Radioactive Cholera

If one more woman tells me what no-'count, wife-beating, insensitive, violent, date-raping slugs men are, and how we're obsessed with the magnitude of our genitals, and fear commitment, and don't have feelings, I'm gonna take a ball bat to her. Then I'll get a Border Collie and a laptop, and go live in a log cabin in West Virginia, and put up signs that say, "Beware of Incurable Radioactive Cholera."

Ha.

What is with women these days? I used to think they were nice people that I couldn't understand, but agreeable and mostly friendly and smiled a lot, and you could dance with them. Lots of them were bright and funny. Most were pretty, which, given that men are dog-butt ugly, made the world a pleasanter place. A guy could talk to women in those days, and it was kind of fun to be nice to them. All in all, I thought they were a splendid idea.

What happened?

Now when I talk to beings of the lady variety, they can't go five minutes without saying something hostile. They can't control it. A man doesn't have to provoke it. If a gal mentions her daughters, she has to let you know that she is raising them "not to need men," and her voice sounds like she had just found an earthworm in her mouth.

Gee, thanks for sharing.

Then she works in the story of her girlfriend who was mistreated by her husband. Next we get that men objectify women, whatever that means, and personally pay them only 56 cents for every dollar a man makes, and victimize them, and only want sex.

Which just isn't true. I also want a restored '57 Chevy with a big-block engine and tuck-and-roll Naugahyde interior. Red.

It verges on hysteria. The other day a high-school girl told me solemnly that five out of seven college girls she met in a dorm room had been raped. Sure. And six of them were space aliens on a package tour from Andromeda.

Dear god and little catfish.

Where does all this loathing for men come from? Yeah, lady, I'm just real terrible. In the morning I get up, throw a few coffee cups against the wall in reflexive rage before killing the neighbor's dog, and then assault a lady accountant from Housing and Urban Development on the subway. The male riders cheer me on: patriarchal bonding. Then we stand around and compare genitals until I get off at the McPherson Square stop. Hey, it's guy stuff.

A lot of this fantasy is just plain nuts. Take the business about men only-wanting-sex. (Incidentally, my stock response is to assume an expression of dispassionate curiosity and say, "Ah. What else have you got?" No, it's not fair. Neither was the original comment. Besides, columnists regard fairness as a sign of weakness.)

Women don't want sex? The second fastest way to lose a woman is to treat her as a sex object. The first fastest is not to. How do you win?

Besides, women look at us as commitment-objects. (Help, I've been objectified.) A guy almost wonders whether he can wait until the second date to get married.

The spooky thing is just how mad most women really seem to be. The dislike is real and profound. And it's one-way. Men don't hate women. They just want to hide.

Best I can tell, women think they're mad because they think they think that men are oppressors and gangsters and thugs. Men think women are blaming everything they don't like in their lives on men. (Actually, men didn't design the world, or anatomy. We came with it.)

The eerie enmity, the apparent belief that everything men do is some technique of oppression to be resisted, seems to pervade everything. You can't see it, but you know it's there, like God and corruption. It begins to have social consequences. Guys ask themselves, "How smart would it be to tie myself to a touchy woman who dislikes my entire species? Why don't I just buy her a house now and skip the intervening agony?"

This sort of thing could almost produce fear of commitment.

I swear it was different in high school and college. Girls were great. Sure, they giggled at some forms of masculine behavior. You know, like bonding with overpowered, under-lubed rustbuckets with glass-pack mufflers and rod knock. The boys wondered why the girls were never on time and didn't want to talk about cam shafts. But there was no venom in it. Now there is.

West Virginia, I tell you. Incurable cholera and all. Radioactive.

13

Blacks and IQ

Let us address straightforwardly a question that is more privately discussed than publicly acknowledged:

As a matter of logic, blacks either (a) are, or (b) are not, as intelligent as whites. For evident reasons, though not necessarily good reasons, people evade the question in public speech. But this is like not telling the doctor about the lump growing somewhere on one's person: current ease of mind exacts the price of later disaster.

The disparity in measured IQ between the races is about fifteen points. If the inequality accurately reflects a real difference in intellectual ability, the consequences will be enormous, for reasons growing out of the overlap of bell-shaped curves. The mathematics is not easily conveyed in a newspaper column. For the moment, suffice it to say that, if the fifteen-point difference means what it purports to mean, blacks, short of a miracle of genetic re-engineering, will be forever excluded from the higher intellectual reaches of a techno-industrial society.

Is the difference real?

First, let us assume that it is not—that is, that blacks are as intelligent as whites. The question then arises: Why in god's name are we not educating black children to the level of white? Blacks lag whites by large margins. If they can perform, the country is criminal in not ensuring that they do.

There can be no acceptable excuse. Children raised half-literate have little prospect in a society that daily becomes more technical. Poor education blights their lives intellectually, economically, emotionally. It also takes a heavy toll on others in crime, the expense of welfare, and lost taxes. It is simply immoral.

Why is schooling so poor for black children? To begin with, because blacks have little enthusiasm for academics. Blacks have demonstrated for an end to discrimination, more welfare, less brutality by police, more rights, more pay, and greater respect. They do not march for more homework, harder courses, thicker texts with larger words and smaller pictures.

Another reason is that the teachers' unions resist the dismissal of the incompetent in a profession that already gets the dregs of the intellectual barrel. Finally, politicians are terrified of blacks, who complain that the imposition of academic standards constitutes a form of imperialism.

Now what?

Second, let us assume that blacks are less intelligent. What can we do?

For starters, we need to recognize that no one is going anywhere. Blacks are not going to go back to Africa. Whites are not going to go back to Europe. We are all where we are going to be. We are not going to turn Georgia, Alabama, and Mississippi into a separate black nation.

Yet neither, if the disparity in intelligence is real, are blacks going to become physicists, engineers, or doctors except in miniscule numbers, or through affirmative action. Leadership, except in electoral office or appointments arising from electoral power, will remain white, engendering resentment among blacks.

Worse, the demand for unskilled and barely schooled labor does not seem to be growing. Already, in a purely economic sense, blacks are unnecessary. They suffer not from discrimination but rather from inutility. They are not persecuted, but ignored. The portents are grim.

Maybe we need to ask—not as a matter of political equivocation or political correctness, but rather as a matter of decency and urgent practicality—whether intelligence should be the prescriptive measure of worth. Blacks have much to contribute that is not mathematics. Musically they are phenomenal, having largely invented this country— jazz, Delta blues, R&B, rock, Dixieland. As entertainers they are wonderful, as athletes incomparable. In years of riding with the police, I've noticed that blacks are better at dealing with people. Maybe these qualities too have a place. We cannot all be computer geeks.

In any event, be they bright or dull, I think we need to arrive at some conclusion—either educate the black population if it can be done, and move them into equality; or, if it can't be done, decide how we may live in comity. People should not be punished for what they irremediably are; nor should the quick-witted necessarily be thought worthy for brains with which they were born.

I sometimes think we are too competitive. American society prizes ability over all else, encouraging athletes to squander their best years in half-mad pursuit of a hundredth of a second in an Olympic footrace. How much sense does it make? Does it really matter whether I am smarter than my neighbor, or he than I? Maybe, if he designs digital signal-processors, and I am a short-order cook, I should buy his stereo gear, and he should eat my hamburgers, and both be content.

14

A Gas-Station View of Evolution

I'm trying to believe in the theory of evolution. It's tough going. I have to squinch up my eyes and imagine hard. But I'm determined to do it, because it's the Right Thing To Do, and keeps people from yelling at you.

Trouble is, I keep running into bumps and potholes.

For example, I worry about The Amoeba In The Soup. We're told that a jillion years ago all sorts of glop and gunch sloshed around in the primeval seas, and *lo!* a wee little amoeba-thingy accidentally assembled itself, the way a car does when you shake a bin of parts. It then evolved furiously into Bill Gates.

OK. Fine by me. I can believe that Bill has amoeboid ancestry. Except: How do we know that the amoeba happened? Other than by blind faith?

Be patient with me. Permit me a few rude questions about the Soup, such as might be asked by a police reporter. Maybe I'm being uncouth, but I don't know any better.

(1) Do we have any evidential reason for believing that the Soup ever existed? Do we, for example, have residual pools of the Soup? Dried deposits somewhere? No. Do we know enough about the formation of planets to know what the soup had to be? No. Then how do we know that the Soup, if any, was the right kind?

Ah. We know it, say evolutionists, because life appeared, which it couldn't have done without the Soup. Therefore the right sort of Soup must have existed.

Good try. But this is reasoning from a previously accepted theory to nonexistent evidence, or, more bluntly, imagining evidence to support a theory that we are determined to believe. Scientifically, this is bad juju. One derives theories from evidence, not evidence from theories. (If memory serves, it is also precisely the Catholic proof of the existence of God: The world is here, something must have created it, therefore God. Or the Soup. Personally, I incline to a primal Salad.)

(2) Well, if we don't know that a workable Soup existed, then surely the formation of life has been demonstrated in the lab? No. You can put various forms of goop and degradation in a flask, and heat it, and run sparks through it. You get chemicals found in living things. You don't get life.

(3) OK. No doubt you can show mathematically that, given time, the amoeba (or Gates) would be likely to form? No, actually. Statistical chemistry isn't that good.

Evolutionists love time. It covers up fundamental implausibilities. All those gazillions of atoms and molecules, sloshing for billions of years. Surely an amoeba would have to clot out of it, if not a bull elephant. *Billions* of years, mind you. Virtually anything would have to form in so much time. No?

Not necessarily. Probabilities can be more daunting than one might expect. Things that seem intuitively likely sometimes just flat aren't. To illustrate the point:

We've all heard Sir James Jeans' assertion that a monkey, typing randomly, would eventually produce all the books in the British Museum. Sound reasonable? Sure, at first glance. But would the monkey in fact ever get even one book?

No. Not in any practical sense.

Consider a thickish book of, say, 200,000 words. By the newspaper estimate that there are on average five letters per word, that's a million letters. What's the likelihood that our monkey, typing randomly (ignoring upper case and punctuation) will get the book in a given string of a million letters?

He has a 1/26 chance of getting the first letter, times a 1/26 chance of the second, and so on. The chance of getting the book in a million characters is one in 26 to the millionth power. I don't have a calculator handy, but we can get an approximation. Since $26=10 \exp(\log 26)$, then $26 \exp(1,000,000)=10 \exp(\log 26 \times 1,000,000)$. Since $\log 10=1$ and $\log 100=2$, $\log 26$ has to be between, somewhere on the low end. Call it 1.2.

The monkey thus has one chance in 12 followed by 1,000,000 zeros. (OK, 999,999 for the picky.) That's what mathematicians call a BLG (Brutishly Large Number). For practical purposes, one divided by that rascal is zero. If you had a billion billion monkeys (more monkeys than *I* want) typing a billion billion letters a second, for a billion billion times the estimated age of the universe ($10 \exp 18$ seconds is commonly given), the chance of getting the book would still be essentially zero.

Now, does the problem of accidentally getting an amoeba involve similar improbabilities? We don't know. A conclusion: Appealing to billions of years of sloshing is not a substitute for knowing what you're talking about.

To sum up all of the foregoing: We don't know that a suitable soup existed. We can't reproduce the evolution of life in the lab, from *any* Soup. And we can't show it to be mathematically plausible.

Might this not be grounds for withholding judgement?

Naw.

Another point—tricky, crucial, and carefully overlooked—is that we don't really know what life is. Evolutionists assume that life is purely chemical: that if we could somehow assemble an artificial cat atom by atom, and then set it to reacting, we would have a genuine, living cat, that would eat mice and miss its litter box. But would we? All known life has come from previous life. Is life merely a complex of chemical reactions? Or is it something that inhabits certain complexes of reactions? Or something else entirely?

We don't know. But we have ample room to suspect that it is something else entirely. Or at least more is involved than chemistry.

Such as consciousness. If anything exists at all, consciousness does. We are all conscious, with the possible exception of network anchormen. Consciousness affects matter: If you will your arm to move, it does. Matter also affects consciousness: If you drop an anvil on your foot, it will decidedly affect your consciousness.

But, though it clearly is an important aspect of life, and clearly influences the physical world, consciousness has no scientific existence, being instrumentally undetectable and having no operational definition. So scientists ignore it.

Ignoring things seems to me a funny way to understand them, but then I always did like my lunch box better than my book bag, and maybe I just don't think right. But I'm still working on believing in evolution. I'll get there. Any day now.

15

The Cultural Vandals Come to Roost

One might be pressed to prove that our country is in fatal decline, but I think a lot of us can smell it. The light dims. Things no longer work. Too many curves point downward, too many of the measures of civilization fail. We bask, still, in the waning sunset of a dying greatness, but it won't last. Maybe our time is over.

A flourishing economy can hide many evils, and does. Computers grow faster, cellular telephones proliferate, and the Internet, perhaps America's last great contribution to the world, advances apace. Employment is high, masking for the moment the rot beneath. Decline, if it comes, as it comes, will be comfortable, a moral and spiritual sump instead of a time of starvation.

Yet it is decline.

Look about. Society coarsens around us. Courtesy withers, vileness flourishes, foul language pours from the radio and the screens that circumscribe our lives, along with witless violence, grotesquerie vying with bloody grotesquerie, with perversion, sadism, and casual murder. We no longer avoid the gutter, but bathe in it. At dinner time, when the young watch, television lovingly portrays a callousness toward death and immorality that makes a Weimar bordello seem a venue of child-like innocence, that calls up the degraded mob in the days of the Roman games.

Our children have never known anything else.

Schooling wanes. The forms of education remain, concealing the vanishing of substance. Daily, word of the catastrophe passes along the Internet. Students in wealthy school districts are discovered to be unable to pass a simple examination in algebra. We find credentialed teachers to be ignorant of their subjects. Our once-great universities give unearned grades to all students, while letting them avoid difficult subjects, while allowing them to pretend to scholarship by taking vacuous majors in Women's Studies and Black Studies. The students rule the universities like barbarians from a dark forest.

The arts have sunk to the level of an amusement park. We have artists of merit, but we honor only blotsters and daubmeisters in our thoroughly silly public prints. Works of sculpture in cold truth often cannot be distinguished from the contents of a junkyard. Language has declined, grammar gone into hiding, the subjunctive disappeared, pride in articulateness given way to something close to shame. The jungle grunting of rap passes for music. Except in technology, the candle of American civilization gutters.

We have somehow lost the gumption to say, "No." To this invertebracy we owe all else. We lack the confidence in our beliefs to tell our children, "You will study algebra and Shakespeare and history because these are the essentials of culture, and because we are your parents and say that you will study them. Ten years hence, you will thank us." We lack the confidence to laugh at inartistic absurdity paraded as aesthetic advancement, or to say that we will not stand for gory dismemberment in cinema. We haven't the will to control crime, to outlaw pornography, to impose ourselves.

Above all, we lack the strength to resist the minorities. This will destroy us.

The best of us cower before the worst. We withdraw into ourselves, into our private lives and families, saying quietly to each other, "It is hopeless." The worst, who do least, grow ever more assertive. They want more. We give it to them.

Instead of saying, "Here are the standards of our civilization. Live up to them," we lower the measures of all things for their convenience. Time and again, monotonously, with the deadening predictability of sunrise, we see that minorities cannot do things, and so to placate them we lower standards for ourselves. If they cannot earn a teaching certificate, we reduce the requirements, and so educate neither our children nor theirs. This folly has become reflexive, dominating discourse, governing policy, instituting a double standard, engendering farce. We judge everything by whether the complaining classes will approve.

We do not learn. The Romans made the mistake two millennia ago of providing free corn to the urban rabble. Soon they had the eternal mob, simmering in the slums, living pointlessly, breeding extravagantly, demanding entertainment and threatening to explode if not pandered to. As with Rome, so with America. Instead of bread and circuses, we provide welfare and television, but the principle is the same. The cruelty of television surpasses that of the gladiatorial games.

Welfare works badly. Charity prolonged becomes charity expected. Demands met encourage further demands. People who contribute little or nothing to society grow accustomed to contributing nothing, and regard leisure as their due. Knowing nothing, they do nothing. And so finally they become superfluous, as society learns to live without them. They are merely there.

The communists prattled of the dictatorship of the proletariat, while practicing the dictatorship of the dictatorship. We have actually achieved the rule of the worst. The unproductive, the dull, the witless, and the shiftless have found that they can marshal more votes than can their betters, and thus they have grasped the levers of power.

Do you find study difficult? Why, demand easier courses, and prevail through numbers. Have the emoluments associated with scholarship and diligence eluded you? Assert that you have suffered discrimination, and hold out your begging bowl.

None dare say, "No." I do not understand why.

Our moral compass no longer functions. Good and Evil have no meaning. A miasmic faith that one should do one's thing, no matter what that thing is, keeps us from making the simplest moral judgements. Where once we believed that the better was preferable to the worse, we now believe that the worse, being more democratic, is preferable to the better. The promulgation of standards has become a sign of elitism, evidence of darkest sin.

Ah, but the rub comes last. We cannot buck, we cannot clamor against the gathering twilight, because of the eerie censorship emanating from everywhere and nowhere, the near-Soviet fear that we will be denounced to the commissariat on vague charges of transgressing vaguer rules. We tremble to struggle. We can lose our jobs if we say anything to offend the protected groups—and everything offends them.

Night is coming, and we are afraid.

16

Elvis His Own Self

You gotta understand the grip Elvis has on the automobile-loving basi-
cally Iro-Celtic libido of the southern United States. Maybe you think
Presley was just the first white rock-n-roll singer. Naw. He's a state of
mind. Anybody who has spent time in the smoky evening fields of the
Mississippi Delta, where people talk slow like sorghum dripping onto
cheap china and mosquitoes gang up in packs and carry off cattle,
knows, just knows, that Elvis is *meaning*. It's in the culture. In fact, it has
been scientifically proved that eating Moon Pies and drinking RC Cola
makes you like Elvis. It's true. MIT did it.

And that's why Elvis will live forever. Especially in grocery stores.

Every time I go to Safeway to buy more of whatever bachelors eat, the
grocery-rack tabloids always have a sighting of Elvis as the third lead.
First comes, "Women With Three Breasts and The Dwarves Who Love
Them." Then there's "Lose Thirty Pounds in a Month While Gorging
Yourself With Chicken Fat." Finally comes, "Elvis Seen Alive In Las
Vegas Or Paris Or the Back Seat Of A Greyhound Leaving Nashville." Or
floating over Graceland in a cloud of light. Or in a flying saucer.

The other night I was on the beltway with a friend who has a Miata in
male-menopause red with awesome speakers. The top was down, the

volume was up, and Jailhouse Rock was celebrating homosexual love among the incarcerated. What more could man born of woman want?

The announcer crooned, "That was Elllll—*viss* the King who may not actually be dead because *yesssss*, he's been seen again according to the AP wire in Mississippi near Tupelo...."

It seemed, the announcer said, that the Mississippi troopers had found some high-school kid and his girlfriend parked naked on a back road at two a.m. with a pile of beer cans on the floorboards. The kid explained that a few hours ago they had left the movies and were driving to the churchyard to think about Jesus together. Suddenly this, like, you know, weird bright *light* from above enveloped their car and they could feel a strange force sucking the car upward.

They found themselves inside a big glowing room like a doctor's office and met with Elvis and then passed out and found they'd been put back on earth on a back road, far from the church. And all those beer cans tossed in. Who would have thought it, space aliens drank Budweiser. They'd probably been experimented on, the kid said, 'cause they found this used condom....

See? Elvis lives.

In the mid-Fifties, when I was a Huck Finn simulacrum of eleven in Limestone County, Alabama, and spent my days eatin' goober peas (known as "peanuts" to the unworthy, chiefly Yankees) out of the fields and letting fly at mosquito hawks with my BB gun, Elvis ruled. I wasn't sure what he ruled, because I hadn't figured girls out yet, but he wafted through everything. I mean, in the seventh grade kids jitterbugged to Hound Dog at lunch and girls, who actually wore bobby socks, carried around magazines with his picture.

People even looked like Elvis. Boys had long Scots-Irish visages with angular facial planes. They looked as if they had been carved with Exacto knives. Most of them had the same hair as Elvis, and practiced letting a cigarette droop from their mouths with a sneering expression (which Elvis didn't, but never mind.) You could tell they had been raised on buttered grits with lots of black pepper sprinkled on top.

Elvis wiggled like he knew about sex, which was thought revolutionary and dangerous because teenagers would never have thought of sex on their own. But pretty soon he was eclipsed by higher forms of expression. It had to happen.

In the Sixties in a club in Austin I saw a band called Klok Mortuary and the Gadarene Swine, consisting of three chords, two bare belly-buttons, and enough hair for a mattress factory. It would have been avant garde if anyone could have spelled it. During the show Klok, an adolescent furball who looked like half a spider, smashed his guitar on the amplifiers, bit the head off a live chicken, and threw the remains to a nest of pet army ants. (I later heard that in Detroit the ants got loose into the crowd, ending the meteoric career of the Swine.) Anyway, the critics were smitten by the performance. It was so...*dynamic*. Klok, who by now had trouble remembering what country he was in, said the chicken expressed his deepest musical thoughts. Which I was prepared to believe.

Anyway, Elvis briefly seemed by comparison as tame as Pat Boone or unflavored Jell-O. But lo, the Sixties passed like a cautious poker player and people noticed that there was something eternal about Elvis. He was good-looking and spoke of heartbreak, love, good dogs, sweet-lovin' women, and poontang. These were things we could all identify with. He came back.

Last week I went to Safeway to get things to heat in the microwave. The first lead on the National Enquirer was, "Midgets, Evicted From Posh Hotel, Honeymoon In Cardboard Box." Next came, "Secret Pentagon Report: Army Growing Dinosaurs To Eat Enemy Soldiers." Finally, "Priscilla Says Elvis Took Nazi Immortality Drug, Drives Pizza Truck In Tupelo."

What did I tell you?

17

The Confederate Flag And The Eternity Of Entitlement

It never stops. On the lobotomy box I once again saw blacks agitating about the Confederate flag. They want it removed, the announcer said, from the official paraphernalia of yet another Southern state. Cleanse those license-plate holders. Purify the evil that lurks in South Carolina. Abolish if possible an entire culture, erase its history, wash away its distinctiveness.

Then, with the predictability of gravitation, the station trotted out a professional black to intone, spare me, that the legacy of slavery required that the flag be discarded.

Why?

Sez me, blacks are citizens as much as anyone else, and entitled to the same privileges, protections, and courtesies as anyone else. That's all they are entitled to. It's all anyone is entitled to. I could get tired of this slavery routine as a justification for anything blacks want. Being a Southern kid, who likes the South, its language, music, manners, and pace, I could get real tired of it.

I suspect I'll get the chance. By all indications, a hundred or a thousand years from now blacks will still be attributing all their problems to slavery. The first rule of American politics has become that everything is someone else's fault.

What are the constant demands by blacks going to do for race relations down the road?

Nothing good. And the last thing this country needs is more racial animosity.

For nigh on fifty years we've been teaching blacks that the way to get anything is to holler about slavery and demand whatever it is. Everybody else has had to work for things. They still do. Indians show up from Bombay and work as programmers, Pakistanis run the Seven-Elevens, the Vietnamese go into the restaurant trade or computational fluid dynamics, Hispanics become construction workers. Blacks by contrast appear to have become a permanent welfare class.

Is this good for anybody? And how did we get here?

Of course what happened was that, after apartheid legally died in the mid-Fifties, all sorts of people figured that blacks needed a social jump-start. It wasn't an unreasonable idea. Further, a lot of people felt guilty about the circumstances in which blacks lived, which were in fact dismal. That sense of guilt too wasn't entirely unreasonable: If whites weren't exactly responsible for an ugly situation, they had at least tolerated it.

Then, when blacks didn't move up the educational ladder, people decided to try a new form of welfare called affirmative action. This lowering of standards for blacks—which is what it was—also was done with the best of intentions. Step by step it went, things being awarded that should have been earned. At the time, nothing else seemed possible. Maybe in fact nothing else was possible.

The result was, however, to teach blacks that all good things come from white people, not from disciplined effort. There came welfare, food stamps, Section Eight housing, and so on, without which today the cities would go up in flames. Then affirmative action, very much a form of welfare, took hold throughout the professions. Blacks now rely on these programs to an extent new to the country.

The reliance may prove dangerous. The position of blacks in America looks to me to be a tottery edifice indeed. Yes, with the economy going well, welfare flows, and yes, with political correctness firmly reigning, nobody can criticize, and yes, with affirmative action, blacks get hired where otherwise they wouldn't be. But...this is precisely the problem. What would happen if anything went wrong? What if there was a serious economic downturn?

Among blacks, there is the powerful sense of entitlement, as well as a hatred of whites. Among whites, a generation has grown up which was born after the movement for civil rights. For them the force of demands for special privilege, based on increasingly remote evils committed by others, diminishes. I recently heard a girl of perhaps fourteen, who had been castigated by black students in her school as a white and therefore guilty of slavery, say firmly to a friend, "I'm sorry, but I wasn't there, and I didn't do it."

What worries me is that the sense of entitlement, the dependence on demanding and on special privilege instead of performance, seems to be increasing instead of dying away. Affirmative action is rampant on campus, in the government, in the military. EEO charges are now a regular way of avoiding complaints about poor performance. In the universities, departments of Afro-American Studies have become entrenched absurdities.

In the short run, nothing is likely to change. The iron grip of political correctness perpetuates the reliance on entitlement. As everyone in almost any office knows, any mention of what is going on will result in getting fired. It is also true that everyone does know what is going on. Here we have the curious two-tier system that has come to prevail in America: What we say publicly, we don't believe, and what we believe, we don't say publicly. The Soviet Union ran on this principle.

But:

If the grip of censorship should fail, should patience with perpetual entitlement end, we are going to have big trouble. The anger of whites is not as intense as that of blacks, or as universal, but there's a lot of it. Not good.

Thing is, we're caught in a Bifurcated Gotcha: On one hand, blacks desperately need to catch up academically and learn to compete with everyone else. On the other hand, as long as we have the system of special privilege, they have little incentive to catch up. If you figure that one out, call. We'll get a patent.

Meanwhile the demands to abolish the Confederate flag, to rename everything named for a Confederate general, or for that matter demands for reparations or elimination of the Declaration of Independence—these are sheer provocation, intended as such. They fan a smoldering resentment among whites that in the long run isn't going to help anyone. If this suppressed anger ever breaks into the open, there's going to be hell to pay.

Maybe we ought to think carefully about it.

18

White Males: Are They Actually Gods?

Tell you what. I'm gonna get me about sixteen Dobermans with no judgment. Then, next time I see one of those chunky talk-show ladies with short hair blowing about what brigands white males are, and how we ought to dethrone them, I'm gonna get the Dobermans to eat her. Then I'll get their stomachs pumped, because I like dogs, and send them on a vacation to the Bahamas.

The other day I heard one of'em blathering about white males. (A chunky lady, not a Doberman.) She was all in an uproar about it. She spoke with the nuanced lyricism I associate with truss ads and said we needed to deconstruct the paradigm of white patriarchal masculinity with its linear-logical gender-hierarchical phallocentric oppressive something-or-other. She wanted to get rid of white males.

I figured she needed to learn English first, but never mind.

Now, mostly I'm a well-mannered fellow, because my momma taught me to be. Sometimes I come up short. This was one of them.

I found myself wanting to say, "Now, listen here, Maple Syrup. You get up in the morning, maybe with the help of a forklift, and get food out of the refrigerator, which white men invented and you don't understand. (What's the compressor for? Did you know a refrigerator had a compressor?) Then you sit down to write your thoughts on a defenseless computer, which white men invented and you don't understand. (What's branch prediction on a floating-point pipeline? Name the three parts of a transistor?)

"Next you to go to the studio in your car, which white men invented and you don't understand. (What are dual overhead cams? The difference between pre-ignition and detonation?) Finally you spew your wormwood and gall on television, which white men invented and you don't understand. (Where is closed-captioning encoded in an NTSC signal? I'll tell you: In the vertical-blanking interval. Now do you know?)

"Hooboy, am I impressed, Sweet Potato. Yes ma'am. I sure enough see why we need to get rid of white males. How could anyone doubt it?"

Actually, I've got nothing against spewing gall. Do a little of it myself. I might spew wormwood too, except I'm not sure what it is. But I begin to notice a pattern. The people who grouse most about white males are people who can't keep up with them, and who owe the most to them. Those who can keep up—Chinese males, Vietnamese males, males from India—don't do a lot of complaining.

Don't misunderstand me. We pale males aren't perfect. Far from it. We've got warts on most of us. We leave things all over the living room. We drink beer and chase women. Sometimes we punch each other out in bars. But we have contributed a few things to civilization. For example:

Euclidean geometry. Parabolic geometry. Hyperbolic geometry. Projective geometry. Differential geometry. Algebra. Limits, continuity, differentiation, integration. Physical chemistry. Organic chemistry. Biochemistry. Classical mechanics. The indeterminacy principle. The wave equation. The Parthenon. The Anabasis. Air conditioning. Number theory. Romanesque architecture. Gothic architecture. Information theory. Entropy. Enthalpy. Every symphony ever written. Pierre Auguste Renoir. The twelve-tone scale. The mathematics behind it, twelfth root of two and all that. S-p hybrid bonding orbitals. The Bohr-Sommerfeld atom. The purine-pyrimidine structure of the DNA ladder. Single-sideband radio. All other radio. Dentistry. The internal-combustion engine. Turbojets. Turbofans. Doppler beam-sharpening. Penicillin. Airplanes. Surgery. The mammogram. The Pill. The condom. The penis. Polio vaccine. The integrated circuit. The computer. Football. Computational fluid dynamics. Tensors. The Constitution. Euripides, Sophocles, Aristophanes, Aeschylus, Homer, Hesiod. Glass. Rubber. Nylon. Roads. Buildings. Elvis. Acetylcholinesterase inhibitors. (OK, that's nerve gas, and maybe we didn't really need it.) Silicone. The automobile. Really weird stuff, like clathrates, Buckyballs, and rotaxanes. The Bible. Bug spray. Diffie-Hellman, public-key cryptography, and RSA. Et cetera.

You're welcome.

Me, I reckon as how radical-feminist ladies can blow their horns as soon as they have a horn to blow. Don't reach for your earplugs just yet. Fact is, being myself a competitive white male, more or less rational, and like most white males inclined to try to figure out this screwy universe and maybe make it a bit less unpleasant for all concerned—I believe I could get along without bitchy feminists. It would be a stretch, but I could do it. The sterile, a curmudgeon might say (though I don't know any of those) have little obvious right to assault the productive, to gripe about what they can't do and can't do without. Fish or cut bait, I might almost say.

Sometimes I think feminism comes down to sheer ill-breeding. When men, as thousands do, (along with any number of women) spend lifetimes in labs at NIH and suchlike, working their guts out trying to find out how oncogenes work and how to get at cancer cells with something they won't like at all—when they do this for thirty years straight, for reasonable but not cosmic salaries—they aren't trying to oppress Native Americans or to batter women or commit incest with defenseless autistics. They're trying to get rid of cancer. The response of anyone with class would be, "Thanks, gang. Keep at it." And when somebody finally does beat cancer, the odds are phenomenal that it will be a white male. Deal with it, Sweet Potato.

Now I've gotta run. To the guard-dog store, for some Dobermans.

19

A Hive of Two-Legged Termites

Political freedom in America differs from Tinkerbell, I sometimes think, in that Tinkerbell just may exist. I submit that the country is not as free as it once was, or as we usually think it is—that we retain the forms of democracy without the substance, a political parlor trick of a high order. And it's getting worse.

Several things got us here:

First, the rise of the judiciary to primacy among the branches of government. The most important decisions are no longer made by elected representatives, over whom we have at least some influence, but by judicial fiat. The courts, and particularly the Supreme Court, enjoy absolute power without accountability. They are now regularly used to impose on the nation policies, often of enormous import, that could never pass in the legislature.

For example the Supreme Court, by discovering a hitherto unnoticed constitutional right to abortion, did what Congress would never have done. (My concern here, incidentally, is not whether these decisions were good or bad, but only that they were brought about without a vote by the citizenry.) Neither could the legislature have passed Brown vs.

the School Board. Nor would Congress have made pornography legal, inutterably coarsening the tone of national life.

Note that whenever the dominant elites dislike a policy passed by a state legislature, they immediately appeal to the courts to have it overturned. Often it works.

Second, the near-total suppression of discussion of politically crucial topics. "Political correctness" was at first a wry expression of annoyance, but has become a national laryngectomy. We now live, as the Russians did, in a society of two tiers of discourse. One tier is what most people think, believe, or know to be true; the other tier is what one is allowed to say. (Observe that almost none of the columns on this site, other than ones about dinosaurs or perhaps boyhood in the South, could be published in any newspaper anyone has ever heard of.)

For example, one may not discuss differences in intelligence between races and sexes, a subject with vast implications for policy; suggest that massive immigration ought to be stopped; point out what feminization of the military is actually doing to the armed forces; suggest that minorities need to behave better and complain less; publish racial breakdowns on sensitive crime statistics; or detail the extremes to which affirmative action has gone in lowering standards. Yes, reasonable people of good will might fall on different sides of these subjects. The point is that debate isn't permitted.

Third, the imposition of reprisals for political incorrectness, and of what amounts to re-education of the recalcitrant in government, the media, the high schools, and the universities. On any campus, and in any office, a remark that offends a black or a feminist is likely to result in reprimands and heavy sanctions. Universities engage in antiwhite racial hazing that is hard to believe, yet students have no escape. The compulsory orthodoxy has ceased being funny and become relentless intimidation.

Fourth, the large size of political jurisdictions, and the concentration of power in remote cities, have sharply reduced our capacity to influence local policy. For example, if you lived in a small town in 1950 and objected, say, to the quality of your children's schools, you could talk to the school board, whom you would know, and the principals and teachers, and the mayor, and have a reasonable chance of getting results with a reasonable expenditure of effort.

Today, the barriers to wielding influence are far higher than they once were. Most school districts are so populous that you probably don't know your elected officials, and they probably don't care about individuals. Ginning up political pressure in a county of 500,000 requires a full-scale campaign, with phone banks, printed flyers, ads in papers, and mass meetings. Few of us have the time.

Further, the real power over schooling (and most other things) lies with bureaucracies far away in the state capital, or at the federal level, or with the national unions of teachers, none of which cares about your kids. Practically speaking, you can't influence distant bureaucracies. They will shrug off your phone call because they know you can't organize the entire nation, that you will eventually give up and go away.

In short, you have the vote, but it doesn't matter.

Fifth, a political system founded on two barely distinguishable parties, an arrangement admirably designed for the suppression of dissent. A parliamentary system, by pooling the national vote for better schools, would allow the election of vocal representatives who would actually pursue the desired end. We by contrast cannot vote for specific policies.

Suppose for example that you favored a sharp increase in academic rigor in the high schools: Advanced courses, decent grammar, teachers who could read. For whom would you vote? What difference would it make? Both parties and all the candidates are vaguely and indistinguishably in favor of better schooling for our children. Neither party has actually done anything about the schools, and neither is likely to do anything.

In sum, as our influence over our lives decreases, as independence diminishes, as the web of rules and regulations and correctness tightens around us, freedom gradually, unnoticed, becomes a thing of the past. In return we get bread and circuses: A startlingly high material standard of living, countless movies to rent, tasteless television dominated by propaganda, rock concerts, ever-better computers, abundant and cheap clothing, and cars that work.

In the long run this may not be a good bargain. Crucial changes in a society are not always evident to those living through them. Romans of the third century didn't know that the Empire was on the way out. We may well be seeing a turning almost as momentous: the end of the United States as a free country, at least in the usual sense of the word, and the imposition of a new form of government: a reasonably benign, and tasteless, dictatorship without a dictator.

Sometimes I wonder whether the Soviet Union so much died as just moved to a different continent, becoming much more comfortable along the way.

20

Interracial Dating

Where I live, the sight of a black guy walking with a (usually blonde) white woman is no longer startling, although many are not at all happy about it. The media celebrate interracial dating as A Good Thing, showing that irrational prejudices are at last dying out and a better world is coming into existence. The national problem is finally going away.

In the long run they may be right. More is involved, though, than boy-meets-girl.

Black men in this country have always been fascinated by white women, at times almost obsessed, because of the forbidden-fruit principle. Until recently, the social message, often explicit, was that blacks weren't good enough to touch a white woman. Bitterness runs deep in black men over this. (This is hardly a secret. Read the first chapter of *Soul On Ice.*)

The social order is now changing. While black men enjoy a new world, black women (if the television specials are right) don't much like it. Although blacks oppose discrimination by color, they have always held to a color code among themselves by which lighter women were better. This preference by their men angers black women—dark women who get overlooked, light ones pursued chiefly for their color, and black women in general, who resent losing, every time. (White women, incidentally, at least some of them, similarly resent Asian women, who charm white men by virtue of their femininity and looks. Asian women, however, are few enough as not to pose a real threat.)

The media and advertising industry understand the color code perfectly. Note how often, when you see a black man and woman on a magazine cover, the woman is lighter. And how few dark women show up at all.

Hostility arises that doesn't meet the eye. On average, white men hate to see black men dating whites. (So do a whole lot of white women.) In places like Washington, people won't say so publicly. Privately they do.

Human behavior usually consists of rational justification of limbic instincts. A powerful instinct of all males is to protect their women from outsiders. People of other colors are outsiders. In slave days, black men were furious that they could not prevent sexual access to their women by white men. Today, the role is being reversed. Black guys know it, and revel in it. White men don't like to admit their resentment because to do so underlines their inability to do anything about it.

It's more than dating. It's potentially explosive sexual competition.

Instincts involving sex aren't always obvious, but they are there, and powerful. An example: I like the Japanese, have great respect for their intelligence individually and for their society (extraordinarily productive, unfailingly courteous, almost free of crime.) Yet if my daughter told me she planned to marry a Japanese boy of impeccable credentials, I'd nonetheless feel a visceral resentment. I wouldn't act on it, but I'd feel it. By contrast, if my son told me he planned to marry a similarly admirable Japanese girl, I'd think he was one lucky guy. The instinct is to protect the women, not the men.

Sex as a weapon of conquest, of struggle for dominance among males, is a dark corner of human behavior that we don't talk about. It exists. Raping the women of one's enemies has been a common military practice until recent times—American armies have done it—and still is if one believes reports from Yugoslavia. White men regularly had their way with slave women, and you can believe that dominance, as well as sex, was involved.

Dinesh D'Souza, the Indian-born scholar now at the American Enterprise Institute, noted in his *The End of Racism*, (page 408, from FBI statistics)…in 1991 there were 100 cases of white rapists assaulting black victims compared with more than 20,000 cases of black rapists attacking white victims—a result that is especially remarkable considering that rapes are usually perpetrated not just for sex but in order to control, dominate, and humiliate women." And also, he doesn't add, their men.

Where white women fit into interracial dating is less clear. Black men are physically more attractive than white, being better built and more muscular—and usually able to beat the stuffing out of white men, which whites of both sexes know. They are also unapologetically masculine (and misogynist, but that can be played down when useful), more assertive, and often charming.

White-collar Caucasian men these days tend to be neutered, carefully inoffensive, and in general browbeaten by militant feminism. It is easy to see how a white woman who wanted a masculine man would find a good-looking black guy appealing. Also, given that white women today seem to dislike white men almost as much as blacks do, dating a black guy may be a way of getting even.

There's a whole lot more going on here than boy-meets-girl.

The media, particularly television and the movies, have recently begun vigorously promoting interracial liaisons. The number of blacks on television in general has risen sharply. Why, I don't know, not being privy to the councils of Hollywood. Perhaps it's just political correctness.

On the other hand, a lot of folk believe that the only way out of our racial impasse is to breed ourselves into one in-between race. Blacks are not going to go back to Africa, say these folk correctly, nor whites to

Europe. Therefore we either blend or stay forever divided. The logic to this point is hard to refute.

Our customary division on racial lines isn't satisfactory, runs this argument. It promotes injustice, and may be dangerous: The country really could go up in flames. Therefore the sooner we intermarry, the sooner our racial antagonisms will disappear. The truth of this theory is much less clear, but is not insane by any means. It seems to be what's being promoted.

Where are we headed? Certainly toward a whole lot more dating and intermarriage: This is a cork that won't go back into the bottle. In the long run, if no explosion occurs, the country will probably evolve toward the example of Brazil. Whether the consequence in the short run will be improvement in racial relations is far less certain.

The effects for a long time will be mainly psychological, as statistically significant blending won't occur soon. Too many blacks live in insular ghettoes, speak Ebonics, and are barely socialized. For them, the prospects of intermarriage are small. The better educated and well-spoken may marry whites, but the vast urban enclaves will remain behind, slowly growing.

Maybe things will work out well. I hope so. But it ain't just true love.

21

An Experimental Novel

"After many a summer we dyed the swan," said the Countess Alexyovna, "but it didn't do much good."

Count Streltzy said nothing. In three days the Kerensky government would fall and all of Russia would be under Bolshevik rule. In the cherry orchard the blossoms dropped, sadly. Drop, drop, drop, they dropped. Alas!

"What color?" asked little Gritchka impulsively.

"What?" asked the Countess, lost in her sorrow.

"The swan, Mommy. What color?"

"Oh, *that*. Puce, I think. Or pimento."

Pablo hitched up his greasy cartridge belt and took a piece of Sauterne cheese from his holster. The cheese was covered with tallow. The Spanish Civil War was going badly. Pablo was on leave from the Catalan front. Spaniards have no regard for chronology.

Count Streltzy said nothing.

"That thou grow tall and straight, little one," said Pablo to Gritchka, "and bear many children, sound of foot. That thou, for whom the Belle Toes...."

"Is that how they talk in Spain?" Gritchka asked. "Is that Spanish?"

Pablo cleaned the cheese with a dirty thumbnail and flicked the tallow to Hannibal, Petrushka's marmoset.

"No. We picked it up from Hemingway. That was before the Falangistas took Halavah."

Baron Kalashnikov was 47 but still a child because of encephalitis. He shouted excitedly, "Tell us more, Uncle Pablo. And was it dangerous?"

"In those years," said Pablo with the dispassion of a man who still has trench-mortar fragments in his leg, "we lived in a wineskin. There was the White Russian, Albinovitch, and the priest, and the cheese. And the corporal with the cast in his eye said, 'That thou blow thy bridges, Pablo. The Little Mule died of his wounds today. That thou blow thy bridges.'"

The petals drifted down, the pale sad butterflies of foreshadowed glimmerings. Count Streltzy stirred restlessly, but said nothing. Ivanitch scratched. Rain fell torrentially around the pavilion.

"It's the monsoon," said the Empress Dowager. "Now the Yangtze will flood. The jade carvings will wash to the sea, and form a delta."

"Still," mused Countess Alexyovna, "our trunks will get to New York, and Gritchka with them. What's the name of the ship?"

"The Titanic," Petrovitch Petrovitch muttered. "It leaves Moscow on the eighth."

He continued leafing through Talleyrand's Anabasis, by Faulkner. Petrovitch Petrovitch was an intense young intellectual of the modern sort, in whose eyes a bitter gleam burned brightly, a beacon beckoning to all who would listen. He yearned to die on the barricades, but there were none in the orchard.

The wind rustled through the cherry trees like the memory of forgotten reminiscences. It made no impression on Prince Mishkin, who was knitting a samovar. He had tuberculosis, as all Russians do.

He said, "As the day in its dawning, so the sands in their shiftings, the blossoms in their droppings. There is a timeless, despondent foreboding in black dreams of a bygone day. Do you sense it? Except perhaps in New Jersey."

Hannibal the marmoset began playing with Count Streltzy's boot laces, but the Count seemed not to notice. He said nothing.

Countess Alexyovna explained, "In New York, they say, the streets are paved with gold. We will have a kiosk on Atlantic Avenue, and sell borscht and beet soup. The marmoset will sit on the roof and eat pigeons. The Empress Dowager will smoke opium and read palms."

"Don't forget the tea leaves. I want to smoke them too," said the Empress.

Gandhi looked up from the notes for the play he was writing and interjected in his thin, sere voice, "Ah."

The wisdom of the orient was contained in the simple remark.

Pablo said, "That there are many bridges in New York. That we shall blow them. For in that year we lived in a culvert, Maria and the Rabbit and I, with the priest and the cheese. The culvert smelled of man sweat and woman sweat and Rabbit sweat, and it was good. The earth was brown and the grass was green. The sky was blue and the water was wet."

Count Streltzy said nothing.

22

Fondling Boy Scouts

I think it was Ulpian, the classical Roman jurist, who enunciated a fundamental principle of jurisprudence: If you put a two-bit lawyer in a black nightgown, you can call him "Judge," but he's still a two-bit lawyer in a black nightie. Which brings us to homosexual Scoutmasters. (Bet you didn't see that coming, did you?)

Anyway, the Supreme Court of New Jersey has ruled that the Boy Scouts must allow homosexuals to be Scoutmasters, joy to pedophiles everywhere. Oh good.

Decisions of this variety are usually couched in terms of civil rights and the duty not to discriminate against homosexuals. This of course isn't the issue at all. The questions are, first, the practical question of whether a figure in authority should be put in charge of children in whom he might have a sexual interest; and, second, the question of sexual privacy: should people be forced to live in intimate contact with those who are sexually interested in them. Homosexuality really has nothing to do with the matter.

First, the practical question: Would we want young sexually obsessed heterosexual males, which is simply to say young heterosexual males, to be in charge of pubescent Girl Scouts? Especially given that Scoutmasters have the moral authority of adults whom, after all, children are accustomed to obey? Do we want sexually active young males sharing tents with girls? Showering? I hope not, because I know exactly what would happen, sooner rather than later.

The difficulty is not that heterosexuals are evil people. The difficulty is that heterosexual males have an intense, clamoring, damned near irresistible interest in female flesh, certainly including that of semi-denuded girls of fourteen. Any man who denies this is lying through his teeth, and all the rest of us males know it.

If you add that girls fairly early learn to provoke such interest, sometimes making a game of it before they are old enough to quite understand what they are doing, you have a recipe for trouble. Society generally is wise enough not to allow men to be tempted by excessively young females. Most men would successfully resist. Some wouldn't. We all understand this.

Do we believe that homosexual males lack a parallel sex drive? That they are somehow immune to the lure of the carnal? Don't kid yourself.

Why then do we think it wise to put homosexuals, who as Scoutmasters enjoy moral authority as well as that stemming from simply being adults, in intimate contact with young boys? Remember that sexually provocative intimacy is the norm in groups of the same sex: A young girl will think twice before parading around nude before a male adult, but a boy of eleven won't.

No, I don't think that homosexuals are particularly inclined toward molesting children, any more that I think heterosexuals are. But I know it to be unwise to offer either group the opportunity. And, while I don't think that most homosexuals are pedophiles, some certainly are—and you don't suppose they would seek out positions as Scoutmasters, do you?

Second, there is the question of sexual privacy. Most of us want to be exposed, sometimes, to people who find us sexually interesting. Most of us want, sometimes, to provoke that interest. Thus we date, flirt, wear uplift bras and tight tee-shirts. The rest of the time we want to be left the hell alone, to avoid the strain of constantly dealing with overtures or the expectation of overtures. This is particularly true of those, notably women, who tend to be the recipients of advances. It is far more true when the advances are made by those whom one finds sexually distasteful.

This is true not only of Boy Scouts. Here, really, is the objection to having the openly homosexual in the military. Men do not like being eyed by other men in the barracks and showers. Pretending that the issue is discrimination rather than sexual privacy makes harder arguing against homosexuality in the barracks, which is why the pretense is made. The reality is that soldiers don't want a gunny sergeant, who they know is gay as an Easter bonnet, who has the power to make life miserable, leering at them if the towel drops.

If I suggested that male soldiers be permitted to shower with the women, everyone would understand without explanation the objections of the females. If I then suggested that I suffered discrimination because I couldn't shower with the women, people would laugh.

But, for reasons that elude me, the objection to unwanted intimacy is thought frivolous if the sexual predator is of the same sex as the prey. It isn't frivolous. Especially when children are involved, it isn't.

As for the Supreme Court of New Jersey, if there were a tax on brains, they would get a rebate. Either that or the members of the court know better and lack the moxie to say so. I worry about men in nighties.

23

Should Voting Be a Felony?

I guess I need my consciousness raised. The newspapers keep fussing and fidgeting because Americans don't vote. Something is wrong with us Gringos, they say. We're shirking. We're no damn good.

Huh?

I look at the last ten or so presidents we've had, and think: hooboy, is *that* what comes of voting? Every one of those reprobates was elected. It's a historical fact. If we can't get any better results by voting, I figure we ought to make it a felony.

How much faith can you put in a system that, out of 280,000,000 people, comes up with Al Gore? Besides, there's the question of culpability. If I voted for one reprehensible nonentity in preference to another, and he won, I would reckon that he was my fault. I don't want a President on my conscience. Further, I do not see how anyone with the slightest self-respect *could* vote.

Anyway, you can't vote for a candidate, because there aren't any. The apparent existence of candidates is a sleight-of-hand.

Do you believe that, say, Gore is a candidate? No. He, like any candidate, is a committee consisting of three speechwriters, a gestures coach, two pollsters, a makeup artist, an image consultant, and several crooked advisers. An alleged candidate is a phantasm, a blank slate or, in the case of Al, a mass of unflavored bean curd.

A candidate is what his advisers tell you he is. Think about it. Often you can read in the *Washington Post* that the candidate, Senator Palmoil, say, is having image problems. Focus groups have discovered, the writer will explain, that he is seen as Insufficiently Manly, that he is not thought by the voters to be adequately decisive, and that his delivery of a speech is positively Caesarian.

The paper will announce that his handlers have decided that he needs to Adjust His Image. That is, Washington's principal organ of misinformation will announce to all the world that the Senator Palmoil is about to pretend to be something he isn't. It will also name the advertising agency hired to perform the mummery.

Sure enough, in his next appearance on television, Palmoil will appear wearing a codpiece. It may have a NOW sticker on it so as not to be threatening to women, and not be excessively protuberant, and perhaps be in an ambiguous beige so as not to be clearly black or white, but it will look no end manly. He will then say Something Decisive, invented for him by the speechwriters and crooked advisers. He will contemplate the teleprompter with an unblinking pole-axed stare, to communicate firmness, and avoid waving his hands around as if he were swatting bugs.

For the next week the talking heads of the Yankee Capital will drone about the effectiveness of the candidate's access of masculinity, about the precise tone of voice in the saying of Something Decisive, and whether the NOW sticker on the codpiece was overkill. In short, the mechanism of deception will be discussed until it collapses into rubble.

Yet, though detailed in advance, though explained in its every calculated nuance, *it will work*. The polls will show that, yes, the Merkun People now believe that Senator Palmoil is of one blood with Clint Eastwood, and that his newly-acquired earnest intonation has satisfied voters of his warm and rich inner life.

I'm going to vote for *that*?

Anyway, you won't know who you're electing until after you have elected him. A campaign is intended to hide the candidate, not to reveal him. The truth is that few candidates have the knowledge or experience to run a Boy Scout picnic.

Occasionally the veil slips. Recently it was revealed that George the Shrub, son of Bush, didn't know the names of the leaders of several mildly important countries. Do you believe that any of them do? The candidates usually are provincial governors, men who have spent their lives crawling up the ladder from law school to county chairman. Why would they know of the likelihood of a Baluchi irredentist movement, or where to find Bishkek?

Now, the professionals of Washington, the reporters and chattering craniums and mechanics of the image trades, do not see things just this way. They take elections seriously, odd though it may seem. They do not understand that they are hucksters playing an elaborate shell game, yet they carefully shield the scam from public gaze. The rule in journalism is that it is acceptable, indeed career-promoting, to trick the candidate into saying something unwise about abortion. It is usually not acceptable to show that he knows far less about the world than most of the reporters covering him.

Note that a news weasel will ask a candidate, "Governor, what is your position on Afghanistan?" The reporter will not ask, "Governor, precisely where is Afghanistan?" The governor will respond to the first question by saying that he favors decency and motherhood, a better life for all Afghans, and human rights for everybody. The response would equally apply to Key Largo or central Illinois. He doesn't know where Afghanistan is.

Oddly, keeping the voters from learning that the candidate does know anything (an unlikely circumstance, but it has happened) is as important as concealing that he doesn't. The voters will resent anyone more intelligent than they are, which we in Washington assume means anyone at all. If a candidate ever mentioned the influence of Sophia of Anhalt-Zerbst as empress of Russia in continuing the policies of modernization of Peter the Great, he would (or so it is feared) lose the election immediately.

The French will elect a man because he is intelligent and cultured. We want someone we can imagine managing a minor Safeway.

A crucial point however is that American elections are not about policy, but about the division of spoils—appointments, contracts, invitations to parties at the White House. Sure, Republicans behave slightly differently from Democrats, but only slightly. Which is to say that elections don't matter.

The economy determines the fate of this country. Presidents don't. They are at worst annoyances and embarrassments, at best a sort of national hobby. What counts is Intel, Microsoft, Boeing, Lucent Technologies, Cisco, AT&T, agribusiness, the Internet. We survive on a strong economic back and a weak governmental mind. Always have, always will.

Vote? Why?

24

Universal Divorce

If you were to believe those unhappy viragos at NOW, you might think that universal divorce was a force for liberation of women, and just a splendid thing for kids. You know the line: marriage is the vilest form of chattel slavery, men molest their kids when they're not beating them like drums, and six out of every four men have sexually assaulted the family dog in the last month. (Actually, I can't think of a better authority on children than 12,000 squalling lesbians who don't have any. Can you?)

Well, let me offer a revisionist view of divorce, from a male point of view:

Cup Cake and Willy Bill get married, because they love each other so. After a few years under one roof, they no longer get along well. Part of it is Willy Bill's fault, and he knows it. Part of it is Cup Cake's fault, but she doesn't know it. She expected more of marriage than it offers. She thought it would fulfill her fantasies and make her happy. It didn't, because married people are just married people, and anyway life ain't all ham hocks and home fries. This too is Willy Bill's fault. Life, that is.

Since Cup Cake wasn't happy being single, and wasn't happy being married, she now figures she'll be happy divorced. She's going to have a dynamite social life, not like living with what's-his-name. She'll have a fascinating job and a swell place. Joe Perfect will appear on a white horse and life will be roses again. She forgets that it never was, and anyway there just isn't that much Prozac. The divorce occurs.

Which devastates the kids. She says it's better for them to have one parent than to have parents who don't get along. This is the Enabling Fantasy of divorce. Ten years later the kids will still be trying to get mommy and daddy back together.

Next, Cup Cake learns that the business world is not importunate in its desire for women of thirty-six with no resume. Day care is expensive. As kids get older, their toys cost more. What's-his-name may have been inadequate as a fantasy mechanic, but he did have a sizable paycheck.

Joe Perfect doesn't show up, which is hardly surprising. Cup Cake isn't Suzy Prom Queen any longer. Most guys shy away from women who always have kids in tow. They have either had kids, and don't want more, or else never wanted them in the first place. As men get older, marriage becomes less important to them.

Cup Cake finds that the men she might date, typically two to eight years older than she is, are a sorry lot. The good ones have been taken. The leftovers are either gay, or confirmed bachelors, or three-time losers looking for their fourth divorce, or such awful dweebs that nobody wanted them in the first place. Or they've been burned in one marriage and aren't about to make *that* mistake again.

In the divorce, either she got the friends or she didn't. When a couple split, the friends seem to think they can continue to be friends with only one of the former couple. If he got them, she's horribly lonely. If he didn't, she finds that married couples, which most of them were, don't want single people around. Four's company; three's a triangle. If she's attractive, it's worse.

Then come the long empty weekends when nobody calls. Depression arrives. She has a hard time growing a new social life because the kids are always there. Depression is two to four times more common in women than men, depending on whose figures you like, and she's got reasons to be depressed. No retirement, for example. She gets a prescription for lithium. Try finding a divorced woman past forty who isn't on Prozac, lithium, Depacote, Zoloft, or Welbutrin, all the M&Ms of the chronically unhappy.

You can't divorce a car payment. Cup Cake finds that she has to have a full-time job, and maybe some part-time jobs too. Days only have twenty-four hours. She doesn't have time to be a full-time mother and have an adult's social life. Often motherhood draws the short straw. She starts leaving young kids alone for long periods while she goes out. By no means all divorced mothers do this, but more do than the newspapers tell you. Latch-keyism becomes inevitable. The kids, unsupervised, feeling neglected, angry because Daddy left, begin to get into trouble.

Not infrequently mommy comes to resent her offspring. They're always there, always whining and fighting and wanting this and that. They make her life miserable, which doesn't happen with two parents, and there's no respite in sight. At best she becomes irritable and seems cold. At worst she slaps the hell out of them.

Then, dear God, puberty hits. Other things being equal, women may be better parents than men for small children. A man would go crazy. For older kids, no. At adolescence they begin asserting themselves and testing Cup Cake. A fifteen-year-old girl makes Genghis Khan look like a milk-fed pansy in lace shorts. With mammals like that, Cup Cake will soon reflect, no wonder the dinosaurs died out. The kids walk over her, becoming contemptuous. She comes close to hating them for it.

A man would say, "No. You aren't going to run away with a feeble-minded dope-dealer who plays bass guitar. Because I say so. We've finished talking about it." It would stick. Women don't do this as well.

Cup Cake's relations with the ex run from none to good. Like as not, she hates him because the divorce didn't make her happy. Frequently she gets back at him through the kids. An angry man smacks someone. A woman's aggression is passive: She withholds sex or, after the divorce, the kids, while earnestly pretending she's doing something else. He gets no influence in raising the tads, doesn't get the report cards or school pictures, isn't consulted.

At best, he gets called only when the kids get into trouble and she can't handle it. Daddy becomes The Heavy. Five years later when they figure it out, they will be grateful. But that's five years off.

And there's nothing he can do about it: "joint custody" or not, if she doesn't comply, his choice is to put up with it, or sue Mommy, which is not the high road to a kid's heart. He puts up with it.

Don't you love it? I mean, what a deal. The kids hate the divorce like poison, Willy Bill misses his kids horribly, and Cup Cake gets to grow old by herself in a bleak apartment with a cat named Fluffy.

If that's not social advance, I don't know what is.

25

A Kennedy Goes Down. BFD.

During all of today there have been weeping and anguish in the media over the demise, in an airplane crash, of John Kennedy, and tearful interviews with people who had no part in it, and quavering by bereaved talk-show hostesses, tremulous with sadness, and assertions by television anchors of our sense, therefore my sense, of loss. As I have listened to this mourning, to this welling up of sorrow, one thought has come again and again to my mind.

Who gives a damn?

By all reports, Kennedy was a half-trained pilot flying over his head in marginal visibility at night over water with two innocent women along. For this, he probably deserved jail time. If he had done it alone, he might have passed as ballsy rather than stupid. Endangering his wife raises misjudgment to the higher plane of immoral irresponsibility.

An outpouring of grief? Why? At best, he contributed to the gene pool by withdrawing from it. At worst, he ought to be prosecuted in absentia.

Why does the country go through paroxysms of weepy Oprah-bereavement over the expiration of unlamentable nonentities? If someone died who had added anything to the world, a Churchill or a Salk or a great blues singer, or a minor blues singer, a degree of distress might be fitting. But Kennedy was just another pampered brat, spoiled rich, perhaps a good husband when not drowning his wife by incompetent flying, but of no obvious concern to anyone outside his family. Why do I have to listen to it?

The Washington Post, ever an embarrassment, intones, "Across Nation, A Sense of Loss and Disbelief." Loss of what? How many of us knew we had him? How many wanted him? What proportion of the public, prior to splashdown, could have distinguished between him and three dozen other Kennedys? What's hard about believing in a plane crash?

I've been forced to listen to this effluvium because the idiot box always runs at the Washington Sailing Marina, where I supervise the Potomac in the afternoon. Over and over I've heard that the Kennedys were "American royalty." Oh? If by this is meant that they were almost as sordid and inconsequential as the British royal family, I agree. Face it: As material for Jerry Springer, Prince Charles is hard to beat. But I don't think this was the intended import.

In fact the Kennedys resemble royalty less than they do the contents of a trailer park, characters suitable for a Faulknerian novel. Joe Kennedy, a crook, bought the presidency for Jack, notorious for cheating on his wife. Bobby was an obnoxious little monster, Teddy a lush, philanderer, and drowner of secretaries, and whatisname an accused rapist. A couple of the Kennedy women, if memory serves, are best known as sots. Maybe they are your royalty. They're not mine.

Does anyone really care outside the media? Do even the media care? I know a lot of reporters, some of them the usual apostles of moral smugness, and none of them will have shed a tear. There is a manufactured quality about the whole affair. We got the same fulsome production when what's-his-other-Kennedy went skiing and made a tree-stop. Not good, but why do I have to hear about it for a week?

It's morally offensive. Around Mexico City, I've seen girls of five years, street urchins, sorting through garbage dumps to find scraps to eat. Pretty it isn't. They're kids, newcomers to the world, who ought to be wearing cute dresses and playing with dolls. Instead they're eating half-decayed slop from tin cans. Sometimes they don't find enough, or some deviate, victim of a bad childhood, catches them alone, and they are found dead in ditches. If the Oprah people want to grieve, let them grieve about these tykes.

In a cab this morning, I heard an alpha-geekess at National Public Radio hanging breathlessly on truly important details, as for example that another piece of wreckage had been found, whoopee-doo, and divers were going down in, oh eek-squeak, eighty feet of water to look for the plane.

Again, who cares? "Look! A fragment of a nacelle. We found it! That'll make things all better." Let an old scuba diver tell you something. When you've spent several days eighty feet under water, you are categorically dead. It's not real reversible. The plane, I promise, is a total write-off. So why do we need unending coverage? Do I need to know about yet another seat cushion?

Tell you what. When my turn comes to go to the great country-and-western bar in the sky, where they two-step until a dawn that doesn't come and the barbecue is succulent with lots of sauce and maybe some garlic, I hope my friends gather to heist a few and remember the good times. Everyone else should be spared. I want my tombstone to say, "Here Lies Fred, Who Was Not American Royalty, And Never, Ever, Went To Hyannis Port."

26

The Weirdness of It All

Times were strange in 1972. Dan and I had just hitchhiked from Thunder Bay in Canada into the main vein of Berkeley. The early afternoon sun was hot and heat shimmered off parked cars in little squiggles. He had a backpack and I had a duffel bag, containing our lives. We had no idea where we were going. In those days it didn't seem to matter.

Dan was a morose Celt who had graduated from college and the Air Force about the time I had finished the Marines. We weren't hippies exactly, but the brooding dissatisfaction of the age lay heavily on us. We'd talked semi-seriously in dorm rooms of paddling into the Okeefenokee Swamp to build a cabin on a hummock and live on tomatoes and watermelons. Trouble was, girls weren't nearly crazy enough to live on tomatoes in a swamp. Anyway the mosquitoes were known to carry off dogs.

The reef life of the Sixties pattered barefoot through the streets of Berkeley. There were student Marxists who had confused their parents with capitalism and were enraged to the gills, and sunburned patriarchs of twenty just in from desert communes, and mind-burnt acid freaks packaging brain damage as mystical insight. Some Hare Krishnas pranced with tambourines in orange sheets and shower shoes from

Dart Drug. Peace, brother, jingle-bang. Oh, and your spare change. Never forget your spare change.

Dan was in a phone booth calling someone in Plattsburg. The connection was bad. I heard him say to the operator, "Platts...no, Platts...no, "p" as in psilocybin...."

She understood. Times were strange in 1972.

Odd things stick in your mind on the road. The high point of the trip had come for me when some librarian-looking lady in a drugstore in Hannibal, Missouri had watched Dan leafing through Playboy. "I think you need a sexual outlet," she sniffed. It was a racy remark for Hannibal. "I've got an outlet," said Dan. "I need a receptacle." Never cross swords with a depressive Irishman.

The roads were strange too. There were places you could hitchhike into but not out of, like black holes. Nobody understood them. One was a place in Canada, called something like Wa Wa, where fifty freaks stayed beside the road for days and couldn't get a ride. The rumor was that some of them had started families.

That night Dan and I found ourselves at a lonely freeway exit curving into nothing a few miles from some Spanish-sounding town—Los Frenos, El Volante, whatever. Traffic died. Nothing moved. The freeway stretched into the night and the quiet was deathly except for the keening of bugs.

We knew we were doomed. In two hours, no car passed. The exit was set between high grassy banks speckled with dispirited trees. Light came from one of those mercury-vapor lamps that made flesh look green and a week dead. High school students used to avoid them because they made acne turn purple.

It was boring. We read the back of the stop sign, where other practitioners of the long-haul thumb had scrawled their sorrows. Little tick marks counted the rideless hours. Five, seven, thirteen. Somebody had written, "Bob died. We buried him under the lindens." I think it was lindens. Anyway, one of those vegetable-sounding words that mean trees.

Somebody had written below, "We killed Chris, and ate him." They probably didn't really.

The hours crawled on like picnic ants. The night grew cooler. We weren't worried. All we had to do was lie down out of sight and go to sleep. A lasting insight of the Sixties was that if you get twenty feet off the nearest sidewalk and lie down out of sight, nobody will know you exist.

Little specks of mica glinted from the concrete. I started thinking they might be lost cities in a science fiction novel, beaming lights upward to signal for rescue. I probably needed my head examined. You can get stir crazy in a black hole.

Dan reached into a cranny in his pack I didn't know was there and pulled out a pint of Jim Beam. "The bar is open," he said. Some men rise to greatness in time of need. We retired to some high grass for the rest of the night. Today we'd be too dignified. I knew we'd never get off that ramp. Ever. Dan wanted to get up the next morning and move in, build a cabin of clay and wattles made. Trouble was, we didn't know what a wattle was.

I don't know how long we lay there, telling tales. The Sixties were an age for tales. I remember telling Dan about the time I thumbed into Riverside to see our friend Jimmy, a musically gifted oddball I used to hop freight trains with along the eastern seaboard. Jimmy was nuts.

Anyway, I'd walked up whatever the main street was. Riverside was a generic pseudo-Spanish Levittown like every freeway stop in California. I was carrying a duffel bag, and began to hear crazy Wehrmacht music from a frame house a block ahead. It was Carmina Burana, and loud. You probably could have heard it on the Mexican border.

In the living room Jimmy was sitting on a section of tree stump. He looked exactly like Rasputin. The walls were plastered with detergent boxes in garish colors. (*"Tide! Bold! Dash!"* What it said about advertising's conception of the housewifely libido, I wasn't sure.) Gilded coil springs dangled from the ceiling. There were six pink porcelain toilets, attached to nothing, in a ring in the middle of the floor.

I asked, "What the hell are these?"

"Toilets."

"I got that far. Why toilets?"

"I stole'em from a hardware store I work at. "

"Ah. But why toilets?"

"They watch everything else."

Somehow it seemed to make sense. Times were strange in 1969.

Anyway, Dan and I actually got out the next morning. An orange pickup with an ardent Marxist stopped and we agreed for a couple of hundred miles that that the dictatorship of the proletariat was at hand, as I've since decided it actually was. Watch any daytime talk show. But we didn't die there on the sidewalk.

27

A Six-Pack, A Bad Mood, and A Typewriter

I begin to weary of the stories about Vietnam veterans that are now in vogue with the newspapers, the stories that dissect the veteran's psyche as if prying apart a laboratory frog—patronizing stories written by style-section reporters who know all there is to know about chocolate mousse, ladies' fashions, and the wonderful desserts that can be made with simple jello. I weary of seeing veterans analyzed and diagnosed and explained by people who share nothing with veterans, by people who, one feels intuitively, would regard it as a harrowing experience to be alone in a backyard.

Week after week the mousse authorities tell us what is wrong with the veteran. The veteran is badly in need of adjustment, they say—lacks balance, needs fine tuning to whatever it is in society that one should be attuned to. What we have here, all agree, with omniscience and veiled condescension, is a victim: The press loves a victim. The veteran has bad dreams, say the jello writers, is alienated, may be hostile, doesn't socialize well—isn't, to be frank, quite right in the head.

But perhaps it is the veteran's head to be right or wrong in, and maybe it makes a difference what memories are in the head. For the jello writers the war was a moral fable on Channel Four, a struggle hinging on Nixon and Joan Baez and the inequities of this or that. I can't be sure. The veterans seem to have missed the war by having been away in Vietnam at the time and do not understand the combat as it raged in the internecine cocktail parties of Georgetown.

Still, to me Vietnam was not what it was to the jello writers, not a ventilation of pious simplisms, not the latest literary interpretation of the domino theory. It left me memories the fashion writers can't imagine. It was the slums of Truong Minh Ky, where dogs' heads floated in pools of green water and three-inch roaches droned in sweltering back-alley rooms and I was happy. Washington knows nothing of hot, whore-rich, beery Truong Minh Ky.

I remember riding the bomb boats up the Mekong to Phnom Penh, with the devilish brown river closing in like a vise and rockets shrieking from the dim jungle to burst against the sandbagged wheelhouse, and crouching below the waterline between the diesel tanks. The mousse authorities do not remember this. I remember the villa on Monivong in Phnom Penh, with Sedlacek, the balding Australian hippie, and Naoki, the crazy freelance combat photographer, and Zoco, the Frenchman, when the night jumped and flickered with the boom of artillery and we listened to Mancini on shortwave and watched Nara dance. Washington's elite do not know Nara. They know much of politicians and of furniture.

If I try to explain what Vietnam meant to me—I haven't for years, and never will again—they grow uneasy at my intensity. "My God," their eyes say, "he sounds as though he liked it over there. Something in the experience clearly snapped an anchoring ligament in his mind and left him with odd cravings, a perverse view of life—nothing dangerous, of course, but…The war did that to them," they say. "War is hell."

Well, yes, they may have something there. When you have seen a peasant mother screaming over several pounds of bright red mush that, thanks to God and a Chicom 107, is no longer precisely her child, you see that Sherman may have been on to something. When you have eaten fish with Khmer troops in charred Cambodian battlefields, where the heat beats down like a soft rubber truncheon and a wretched stink comes from shallow graves, no particular leap of imagination is necessary to notice that war is no paradise. I cannot say that the jello writers are wrong in their understanding of war. But somehow I don't like hearing pieties about the war from these sleek, wise people who never saw it.

There were, of course, veterans and veterans. Some hated the war, some didn't. Some went around the bend down in IV Corps, where leeches dropped softly down collars like green sausages and death erupted unexpected from the ungodly foliage. To men in the elite groups—the Seals, Special Forces, Recondos, and Lurps who spent years in the Khmer bush, low to the ground where the ants bit hard—the war was a game with stakes high enough to engage their attention. They liked to play.

To many of us there, the war was the best time of our lives, almost the only time. We loved it because in those days we were alive, life was intense, the pungent hours passed fast over the central event of the age and the howling jets appeased the terrible boredom of existence. Psychologists, high priests of the mean, say that boredom is a symptom of maladjustment; maybe, but boredom has been around longer than psychologists have.

The jello writers would say we are mad to remember fondly anything about Nixon's war that Kennedy started. They do not remember the shuddering flight of a helicopter high over glowing green jungle that spread beneath us like a frozen sea. They never made the low runs a foot above treetops along paths that led like rivers through branches clawing at the skids, never peered down into murky clearings and bubbling swamps of sucking snake-ridden muck. They do not remember monsoon mornings in the highlands where dragons of mist twisted in the valleys, coiling lazily on themselves, puffing up and swallowing whole villages in their dank breath. The mousse men do not remember driving before dawn to Red Beach, when the headlights in the blackness caught ghostly shapes, maybe VC, thin yellow men mushroomheaded in the night, bicycling along the alien roads. As nearly as I can tell, jello writers do not remember anything.

Then it was over. The veterans came home. Suddenly the world seemed to stop dead in the water. Suddenly the slant-eyed hookers were gone, and the gunships and the wild drunken nights in places that the jello writers can't imagine. Suddenly the veterans were among soft, proper people who knew nothing of what they had done and what they had seen, and who, truth be told, didn't much like them.

Nor did some of us much like the people at home—though it was not at first a conscious distaste. Men came home with wounds and terrible memories and dead friends to be greeted by that squalling she-ass of Tom Hayden's, to find a country that, having sent them to Vietnam, now viewed them as criminals for having been there. Slowly, to more men than will admit to it, the thought came: "These are the people I fought for?" And so we lost a country.

We looked around us with new eyes and saw that, in a sense the mousse people could never understand, we had lost even our dignity. I remember a marine corporal at Bethesda Naval Hospital who, while his wounds healed, had to run errands for the nurses, last year's co-eds. "A hell of a bust," he said with the military's sardonic economy of language. "Machine gunner to messenger boy."

It wasn't exactly that we didn't fit. Rather, we saw what there was to fit with—and recoiled. We sought jobs, but found offices where countless bureaucrats shuffled papers at long rows of desks, like battery hens awaiting the laying urge, their bellies billowing over their belts. Some of us joined them but some, in different ways, fled. A gunship pilot of my acquaintance took to the law, and to drink, and spent five years discovering that he really wanted to be in Rhodesia. Others went back into the death-in-the-bushes outfits, where the hard old rules still held. I drifted across Asia, Mexico, Wyoming, hitchhiking and sleeping in ditches until I learned that aberrant behavior, when written about, is literature.

The jello writers were quickly upon us. We were morose, they said, sullen. We acted strangely at parties, sat silently in corners and watched with noncommittal stares. Mentally, said the fashion experts, we hadn't made the trip home.

It didn't occur to them that we just had nothing to say about jello. Desserts mean little to men who have lain in dark rifle pits over Happy Valley in rainy season, watching mortar flares tremble in low-lying clouds that flickered like the face of God, while safeties clicked off along the wire and amtracs rumbled into alert idles, coughing and waiting.

Once, after the GIs had left Saigon, I came out of a bar on Cach Mang and saw a veteran with a sign on his jacket: VIETNAM: IF YOU HAVEN'T BEEN THERE, SHUT THE FUCK UP. Maybe, just maybe, he had something.

This piece originally appeared in Harper's magazine. Reprinted with permission.

28

Fly, Bossy, Fly!

Once I told my old man that I couldn't understand social policy. I guessed it was because I was young and dumb and lived up the holler where we didn't have any.

"Son," he said, "You can't get milk from a turkey buzzard."

He understood social policy.

The way the old man figured, some things are what they are, and that's all they're ever going to be. There's not much hope in trying to get a spotted cow to nest in trees and lay eggs. A vulture and a cow are just different things. Their approaches to life aren't the same.

You can get paper mache and Elmer's Glue, and stick wings on old Bossy, and get her up to a good trot to get some air under the wings— but she still ain't gonna fly. You can say she'd be a turkey vulture if her childhood had been different, maybe if she'd grown up in a non-patri- archal gender-neutral non-linear-thinking society with lots of drum- ming circles and holistic food—but she'll still be a cow. You can get a crane and balance her in trees and give her Ritalin so she'll think she's a vulture and raise her in a zoo full of vultures to set an example. Won't work. You'll just get a messed-up Guernsey.

It looks to me like our social policy mostly wants vultures to give milk.

The scallawags who run what used to be this country seem to think that all people are the same, except for how they're brought up. Men and women, girls and boys, blacks and whites and browns, turnips and okra and tadpoles. All you have to do is tinker with their upbringing some, and you'll get interchangeable units who'll vote Democratic.

I expect it'll work. Probably about a week after the Second Coming.

A while back I was at a picnic where they had little kids running around and tearing things up.

Well, the girls sat under a tree and played with dolls, real peaceful. The boys tore things up.

One little terror had a complicated twelve-color plastic squirt gun with a banana clip full of nuclear

death-rockets and a laser space-alien disintegrator and a Doppler radar sight with beam-sharpening and lots

of funny knobs. It was about as big as he was. He jumped into the middle of the grown-ups in a Sergeant

Rock pose and yelled, "I shoot you all!"

Boy kid. I don't think pink booties would have helped. He knew we were dangerous pod-people come to wrap earthlings in spider webs, and he was going to protect the planet.

Not long ago I saw the same kid. They'd put him on Ritalin or some other kind of dope, and he was...very...quiet. Which was too bad, because his real problem was that his mother was an unmarried lush who didn't know to manage a little boy. Point is, we've got the entire establishment of teachers, psychotherapists, and purple-haired lesbians wanting to make little boys into little girls. You can't do it. All you'll get is a messed-up little boy.

If he were my kid, I might wonder what ten years of politically motivated pharmaceuticals would have on his brain chemistry, but this isn't a question that gravely concerns feminists. They, in an uncharacteristic concession to decency, are sterile as mules, and can't tell a kid from a summer melon. But they're sure willing to tell us how to raise them.

Now, anyone with the brains of a can of paint knows that a boy's energy and assertiveness and adventurousness and fascination with things that have lots of knobs is what, later in life, will produce DNA sequencers, symphonies, and Mars probes. If you were to look at who invented the things that allow cantankerous lesbians to complain in comfort, you might notice a pattern. Probably it wouldn't be a gender-neutral pattern.

Today we're hell-bent on making people by sheer assertion into what they aren't, and can't be, and probably shouldn't be. It's not just making boys into girls. I keep reading about how the Federal government is going to go after Silicon Valley because it doesn't have enough black chip-designers.

Of course it doesn't. You can't hire the which there ain't. It's a law of nature. Same thing happened when I used to cover defense. Contractors were supposed to hire fifteen percent black laser physicists, of which the entire country had about one. He could have had forty-seven jobs at once but the hours would have been awful, and don't even think about the commutes.

Best I can tell, there isn't the slightest sign that there ever will be many black laser physicists. Maybe it isn't something they do. If some can, and want to, that's fine by me. I just haven't seen it.

Men and women are like that, too. They're just different, and they do different things. You can get a man to chop cordwood all morning, and dig ditches and grunt and sweat, and build barns and carry big heavy awkward stuff, just like it was sensible. He'll unload trucks and change bearings on a diesel. He doesn't know any better. It's how men are.

But it's rough getting him to change diapers. He usually can't nurse real well either, and mostly doesn't know where he left his socks, and thinks the middle of the floor is a perfectly good place for his scuba gear and filter wrench. That way he can find them.

Reckon maybe it's built in?

No. That's too easy. We can't let people be what they are. Instead we believe that if you insist hard enough on some damn-fool notion, and pretend, and swear it's true and claim it's working and sue anyone who sees it isn't, and hold your breath and turn blue, people will be whatever you want them to be. Maybe they won't. The species has always been more than a mite intractable. Maybe it's time we noticed that people just flat aren't the same, and learned to live with it. Because we're going to live with it anyway.

Something needs to change. If people can't figure out what they are, and get used to it, the world's gonna be funnier than when Aunt May sat on the ant's nest. And poor old Bossy won't ever be comfortable up amidst the pinecones, or ever manage to get the hang of laying eggs.

29

Thinking About Fernando

Regarding the enormous influx of Hispanics into the United States through Mexico, a few disordered and chaotic thoughts:

To begin with, why does it get so little attention? The flow across the border is huge, 1066 by inadvertence, resembling the movement of the Germanic people into the Roman Empire in the fourth and fifth centuries. We no longer control our borders. As more Mexicans arrive, their growing political influence will ensure that we will be unable to reassert control.

When the migration has finished, the United States will be a very different place. Whether the change will be good or bad can be debated. That it is a watershed in our history cannot. Why so little discussion?

Answer: Political correctness. Unfavorable commentary on immigration is almost unpublishable.

Next, who are these new folk? What are they like?

I can give you my own anecdotal answer. I've lived in Mexico, and watch the Spanish channels on cable to keep my Spanish up. These provide a window on the Hispanic world. To my eye, Mexicans (though this is less true of the Spanish-speaking Indians who make up much of the influx) are remarkably like mainstream white Americans. They feel

European, not surprising since they are Spanish in origin. Their talk shows and game shows are exactly like ours, the same soft porn and relationships. Their attitudes toward most things are similar to ours. I see no obvious reason why they should have any greater difficulty melding than did the Italians.

Unlike blacks, Hispanics are not angry at the United States. They very much want to be here. You couldn't drag them back across the border with a backhoe and a team of mules. They constantly talk about having come here to find "*una vida mejor*," a better life. When you've lived under the Guatemalan police, you have no doubts about the superiority of San Diego.

They want to be not just in the US, but a part of it. A standard topic for news features is that some Hispanic has made it in America, and boy are we proud. When a Hispanic singer "crosses over" (i.e., manages to become popular with Anglo audiences) the Spanish channels are no end pleased. Every Spanish-speaking actor who gets a part in a movie in Hollywood is chronicled: Hey, we're getting there. Sammy Sosa was to them evidence that they are becoming part of America.

They clearly think that they have a right to be in this country, regardless of what Anglos want, and vigorously support immigration. It isn't a rational view, and infuriates a lot of Anglos, but they hold it tightly. This is the Promised Land, where the poor and oppressed can have a better life. They have a right to come if they choose.

Don't waste your time arguing with them. You won't win.

Hispanics think politically, know they are gaining political power, and plan to use it—not against Anglos, against whom they have little, but for Hispanics. The election of Hispanic officials is very much noted. There is a political vitality to these people that one does not find in, say, blacks, with whom they see themselves as being in competition. (They don't quite say this. Over and over, though, they point out that in a few years they will be the largest ethnic minority in the nation.)

The Hispanic-black competition may heat up. Already around Washington blacks are angry that Hispanics are taking what blacks regard as their jobs. The Hispanics are going to win this one. People who hire uneducated labor routinely tell me that they prefer Hispanics because they show up on time, don't call in sick or simply not appear, don't have bad attitudes, and work like dogs. Guess who they hire?

Hispanics do not want to be linguistically isolated, do not want to turn the United States into a nation divided by language. The Spanish channels groan under the weight of commercials for instruction in English. In the typical ad, Jose gets turned down for a job or a date with an Anglo lovely because he can't speak English. After going to the school being advertised, he has a job in a bank. They are not enthusiastic about bilingual education. The activists are, but people interviewed in the street invariably say they want their kids to learn English, right now if not sooner.

Spanish, not English, is the endangered language. On talk shows in Spanish, such as "Christina" out of Miami, younger guests often have to ask how to say things in Spanish. A joke in English gets a laugh from the audience. When they drop in English words, which they often do, the accent is usually perfect: English is their primary language, or at least equal to Spanish. Believe it or not, several times I've heard Hispanics arguing for bilingual education so that their kids will learn Spanish, which many are forgetting.

As a police reporter, one of my other guises, I see a lot of Hispanics. Here the picture differs a bit from the view on television. The elder Hispanics are friendly, courteous to the police, and do not engage in serious crime. You can find exceptions, but the foregoing is the rule. They tend to drink hard, however, and account for a high proportion of drunk drivers—and I mean drunk sometimes to the point of bouncing from curb to curb. Friends at detox centers talk of seeing blood-alcohol concentrations that would pickle most people.

More ominous, the kids do not seem to be academically ambitious or inclined to work hard. They drop out of school, don't show much interest while they are still in, and, at least around Washington, join suburban gangs. These are not hardcore gangs like the Latin Kings in Chicago, but they aren't good either. If Hispanics are not going to become at least partly stuck in the lower rungs of society, they had better get over the lack of interest in school. No promises there.

The overall prognosis? For what it's worth, my take is that they'll make it. The road may be rocky at times, but they'll get there. I think. The odd cultural barrier that exists between blacks and whites does not exist between Anglos and Hispanics. They'll move up, fit in, mix. (Leave the latter to young Anglo guys.)

I'd better be right, because they're not leaving.

30

Decrypting Gun Control

If you were to trust the media, truly never a wise thing to do, you might believe the controversy over gun-control to be a Manichean dispute between shadowy fascists and an angelic horde. Journalism is ever the dark night of the mind. The anti-gun crowd believe the other side consists of heartless Bull Conner clones who want to shoot orphans, widows, and people in wheel chairs. The pro-gun folk, who at times can be almost equally silly, think that the other side wants to make the nation into a communist dictatorship.

Actually, good and evil have little to do with it. The debate over guns is a clash of cultures, a confrontation of different kinds of character, a disagreement over social philosophy, and even—though few notice this—over free will and determinism. The contending factions don't need guns to detest each other. They would anyway.

Those who favor free ownership of firearms tend to be rural, from the South or West, tough-minded, self-reliant, and disposed to believe in personal responsibility—i.e., free will. Those opposed are usually urban or suburban, more northerly and easterly, unacquainted with self-reliance, tender-minded, and inclined to believe in determinism—i.e., that society determines our behavior. Exceptions can be found in droves, yes. Western megalopolitans may oppose ownership of guns, while New Yorkers from small towns may not. But the foregoing dichotomies establish the poles of the debate.

The two sides have entirely different views of the world. In their approach to guns, both are expressing their experience. They hate each other.

Let's start with the outlook of the pro-gun folk. I know them well, having grown up in rural Virginia. Everybody had guns, certainly including me. (A lovely Marlin lever-action .22.) Kids of fifteen bought ammunition at any country store, and no one thought anything of it. The first day of deer season was a high-school holiday, since the teachers knew that the boys weren't going to be there anyway.

Guns were several things to us. To people who often lived at the low end of the lower middle class, the shooting of ninety pounds of dressed venison was not trivial. Farmers used guns to kill whistle pigs that ate crops. Shooting was sport. Guns and dogs a source of protection in lonely homes. For a boy, getting a first gun was a rite of passage to adulthood, or toward it, like a driver's license or a girl's first bra. Though few recognized it, guns symbolized the independence that rural people prize.

There was almost no crime, and no gun crime at all. We shot rats, deer, beer cans, frogs, and golf balls. (Well, I did.) We didn't shoot each other. We didn't think about it. There were things you just didn't do. When two kids settled a dispute in the boy's room, bloody noses and puffy eyes abounded. Nobody—ever—kicked the other guy in the head, picked up a piece of pipe, or went for a gun.

People viewed crime as a choice. Nobody made you rob a bank. You did it because you decided to. Personal responsibility. Guns? We had lot of guns. We had no crime. Therefore guns didn't cause crime. *Quod erat demonstrandum.* Any fool could see it.

Now consider those who oppose guns. They live in urban agglomerations where people exercise little control over their circumstances.

They are accustomed to relying on the group instead of on themselves. Police provide protection, the plumber changes washers, Safeway supplies food, a mechanic does things with the alternator whazzit. Contractors build the addition to the house. Dependence on others is the rule.

Theirs is a society of the tender-minded, inclined toward organized compassion instead of toward gutting it out, a land of therapy, support groups, and the detailed study of feelings. Having little sense of individual control over destiny, their lives narrowly bounded by the rules and regulations needed in mass society, heavily psychologized and Oprahficated, they lean toward believing that we do what we do because of society's influence. You rob a bank because of your upbringing.

No personal responsibility.

To them, crime is like the weather: something one suffers rather than something one does anything about. Criminals in cities are too numerous to be suppressed except by harsh measures which, aside from being unconstitutional, do not appeal to the tender-minded. Criminals, they believe, can't be held to civilized standards of behavior. So, they reason, we should take their guns away, and they won't shoot each other.

Which of the two views of existence is correct, if either, I don't know. If I had been raised in the ghetto, I'd probably be a drug dealer. But that's what the dispute is about.

There is, of course, more than the cultural divide behind the dispute. The unspoken subtext of debate over guns, always, is race. Whites are terrified of blacks. When their first kid reaches school age, white parents move to the whiter suburbs—liberals as quickly as conservatives. When whites think about armed robbers, rapists, or burglars coming through the window in the night, they think about blacks. The statistics bear them out. The carnage in the cities, for example, is almost entirely committed by blacks against blacks.

But no one dares mention race. For liberals—though they fear blacks and flee from them: look where they live—there is a powerful ideological aversion, forged in the anti-apartheid movement of the Sixties, to criticizing blacks. The black vote is crucial to Democrats in presidential elections. Reporters keep their heads down: The chains of political correctness are real and strong. You can lose your job by saying the wrong things. Consequently what writers say, we don't believe, and what we believe, we don't say.

If you fear crime, yet can't attack the criminals without seeming to be racist, and either can't or won't do anything practical about racial ills, then you attack guns. There is no political penalty. (Oddly, the recent series of multiple murders in the high schools and elsewhere have been a godsend for people opposed to guns because the killers have been almost entirely white.)

That, it sez here, is the reality of gun-control.

31

A Plague of Grief Therapy

I reckon we ought to find an abandoned oil well in some forsaken part of Oklahoma, way out where tumble weeds bounce around all lonely and nobody ever goes. Then we'll canvass the country, and find all the grief therapists, and stuff them into the well. Then we'll pour a concrete plug on top of 'em, and a thick layer of potassium cyanide.

Then we'll eat ribs and drink beer.

Ha.

I can't figure it. Used to be, if an earthquake happened and Granny got squashed, and your town was pretty much flat, you felt bad about it. You probably felt real bad. But feeling bad wasn't practical, so you held yourself together, dug through the rubble for the living, and buried the dead. Next you sought solace in God, philosophy, or a bottle, depending on taste. Then you built another town.

I don't guess it was fun. I don't guess it was easy. On the other hand, nobody thought life was a rose garden. It wasn't in the contract. So you said a man's gotta do what a man's gotta do, and did it. (And yeah, so did women. But the Duke didn't mention women.)

That was then. Nowadays when a tornado hits a trailer park (tornadoes all do: they just seem to like trailer parks) the first thing that arrives is a passle of grief therapists. They're the new ambulance chasers. They come like blowflies to help you process your issues.

Ain't it hell? Your new double-wide is all in flinders across the highway. The last you saw of your wife and dog, they were going up the funnel. Now some patronizing little wart in librarian glasses is telling you it's ok to feel your grief.

I'd kill'em.

I mean, when something lousy has happened, and you've got to scrape up the wreckage and get on with life as best you can—how much do you need a solemn dweeb with a degree in psychology? A wheelbarrow, yes. Maybe a backhoe and some paramedics. A ham sandwich and hot coffee help in most emergencies. But—a *psychology major*?

I tell you, it's the Oprafication of America. Know all those talk shows with ugly fat women waggling their feelings at you—Oprah, Ricci Lake, Jerry Springer—and generally humiliating themselves? They want the whole country to do it. And they're making it stick. We're ruled by gelatinous talk-show hosts. We're turning into them.

What I want to know is where grief therapists come from. They seem to pop up at disasters faster than toadstools in damp weather, almost before the medical folk show up. Do they somehow come *with* tornadoes, in a package deal? The victims go up the spout, and the grief therapists come down it? Are there central warehouses full of therapists, stacked like cordwood, or maybe stored in Cosmoline, waiting for The Call?

Hey, this is pretty scary. The country may be riddled with grief therapists. Like grubs in a rotting tree.

And who pays for them? Did anyone ask whether you needed any grief therapists, and tell you how much these earnest tadpoles would cost per each? I'll bet you there's a federal grant in the woodwork somewhere. Uncle Sucker will pay for anything.

What worries me is, it may be a conspiracy by space aliens. Right now, if a bunch of space aliens landed and tried to take over the world, guys would run out and smack'em with ball bats. The space aliens wouldn't like it. But if they can get us to whinny and whimper instead, and get into grief circles, and share, and validate each other's feelings, then they can turn us into pod people or larvae or something in about ten minutes.

If you didn't know space aliens were behind it, you'd figure we were in the middle of some weird celebration of gooberish weakness. Time was, it was thought adult and responsible and manly to take care of yourself. If your house fell down, you put it back up. If a drooling drug-crazed pervert rapist with a butcher knife came through your window at night, you shot him and got the rug cleaned. Sobbing and glubbing and complaining were looked down on.

It seemed to work

Today, if a guy doesn't fall apart in the most embarrassing manner you can imagine, under the mildest stress, some earnest grief-counseling geekess will tell him that men need to get in touch with their feelings. (Men devoutly wish women would get out of touch with theirs.)

We have a different flavor of therapist for every contingency. See, it's multi-faceted, specialized, categorized patheticness. (That was almost a word.) Look in the self-help section of any bookstore, and you'll find titles like, "The Agony of Limp Hair: A Guide to Recovery." So help me, I've seen "pet-loss grief therapy" on the lobotomy box. Your cat croaks, so a dweebette appears, solicitous and consoling enough to gag a maggot, to help you work through your grief.

Over a cat.

Now, you'd think an adult could survive cat loss without a support group. Sure, Tabby was an agreeable animal and purred when cosseted. Cats aren't evil. They're just useless. And now Tabby is gone forever—in heaven, ignoring God. There's a sense of loss, I guess, like when you misplace your keys.

But—a grief therapist? To tell you not to spend too much time alone at first, especially at night, and don't dwell on things that were dear to

Tabby, like her ball of string, and her catnip mouse, and her half-eaten roaches? And remember when you get a new kitten, don't think of it as a replacement for Tabby who is irreplaceable in your heart, but rather et cetera ad nauseam and beyond.

They talk like this, so help me.

Stuff'em down a well, I say. Shove Oprah on top, like a cork. And then go for barbecued ribs.

And lots of beer. We'll need it.

32

A Nation of Geldings

Ever wonder why masculine men are dying out—the old strong, silent type who rolled cheroots one-handed while roping dogies with the other—and being replaced by delicate androgynous Ken-dolls who look like Tinkerbell with a flat chest? Or why women look increasingly…not masculine so much as sexless?

Tell you what I think.

I'll bet that surprises you.

Used to be, men and women were different, and they knew it. They weren't in competition. So a guy could be Marlboro Man, or sort of anyhow, and grunt, and stand tall in the saddle, and say, "Hoo-*ahhhh*!" and ride Harleys. And if anybody messed with his kids or women, he'd take a tire iron to'em, or a thirty-thirty, depending—or at least imagine that he might. He had sense enough, anyway, to know that it was a good idea.

Back then, a woman could like a big hairy-chested hunk, because she wasn't competing with him. In fact, the hairier and chesteder he was, the better, because she was vying with her girlfriends to see who could get the manlier man. And a lot of women liked the idea of 240 pounds of muscle in a Stetson that meant to take care of them.

She meanwhile could afford to be cute, feminine, and curved, and dress like a woman, and maybe wield a gorgeous smile that she used to play him like a banjo—which he probably knew, and figured that was OK too, because that's how things worked, and anyway guys are guys. She didn't have to out-hairy him. She wasn't trying to be a guy.

East was east, and west was west, and the twain would meet at the drop of a hat.

Then everything changed. Women decided they wanted to compete with men. OK. I can understand it. If I were a woman with an IQ of 160, I'd probably want to be a biochemist instead of child-herd and doily-polisher. The idea seemed reasonable to most women, and to most men. A kajillion gals poured into the workplace.

Thing was—and nobody had really thought this out—they didn't expect to compete on their merits as individuals, get as far as they got, and figure that was the hand God dealt them. They wanted to duke it out head-to-head, self-consciously and avowedly, as a class, with men. It wasn't Sally wrestling with the law boards. It was Us agin' Them.

Which was a Whole Nuther Thing. No society or species had ever tried it.

Problems arose. Fact is, men are hard to compete with. Physically, they are taller, heavier, much stronger, more durable and more enduring. Except for nymphet gymnastics, there may be no sport in which women hold the record. Intellectually men have a large advantage mathematically and a slight one verbally at the high end, that becomes rapidly greater as one moves to the right of the mean; This is the Glass Ceiling. Men are more aggressive, exploratory, adventurous, and versatile. Sorry, but there it is.

Women moved up some, and some moved up a lot, but they didn't catch up numerically with men. It was because they couldn't, and that's a pretty good reason. And when you got down to it, women just didn't care enough. They had other things on their minds, like families and rugrats.

They didn't quite understand this. Nobody did. All women wanted, they said early on, was to be judged by the same standards as men. It was a bad idea. If I judge Sally Sue as a woman, I note that she is sleek, smart, funny, graceful, sweet as sorghum on a Moon Pie, and dances like a dream raised in Arkansas. I'm smitten.

If I judge her as I judge men, she's an emotionally unstable dwarf. How much respect am I supposed to have for a 5'3" guy who bench presses a twenty-ounce Pepsi?

Antagonism inevitably ensued. Men said that the ladies didn't want to be women, and couldn't be men. Why, they asked each other, did a first-rate woman want to be a second-rate man? The women said men were bigoted. Men said they were just observant. Women, who had always regarded men as commitment objects and pre-med objects, became enraged that men regarded them as sex objects. Men were puzzled. They didn't know what else to regard as sex objects.

I was confused myself. I remember a woman screaming at me, "Women don't want to be objects!" Trying to be conciliatory, I said, "OK, you can be subjects." That didn't suit her either.

They don't know what they want. And that's the problem.

They got angry and developed chips on their shoulder pads. War ensued, in which women raged and men didn't know what the hell was going on. When natural ability failed, women discovered, politics would serve. And so we got affirmative action, which means, "pretending."

Depending on the venue, the women needed very little or lots of pretending. The military was worst. It pretended either that women could climb obstacles, or that wars didn't involve obstacles. Soon soldiers discovered that most women couldn't throw a grenade beyond its bursting radius. This will make you unpopular on battlefields. Besides, a woman throwing a grenade looked like a sea lion waving its flipper. So the Army built a little wall for them to drop grenades over.

It was ridiculous. It is ridiculous. Affirmative action always is. Nobody is fooled. Still, it spread like peanut butter on a hot day. For those women who didn't like men anyway, it was sweet revenge. Except—it wasn't quite. The men knew, and the women knew they knew. On the other hand, the checks cashed.

Intuitively women knew they had to push for unisex. To compete with men, women had to act like men, who are competitive, and get men to behave like women, who aren't. They bought ugly sexless suits, did boring things with their hair, and practiced being disagreeable, often succeeding wildly. Meanwhile the media, fronting for them, went in for pretty male models who waxed their chests and weren't threatening. The compassionate man emerged like a grub from a log.

The women won. Marlboro Man, or anybody too clearly of one sex or the other, is out of style. Both the New-Age woman, and her docile man-surrogate, would be intimidated, and ol' Marlboro would have trouble knowing which was the girl.

God it's boring.

33

I Was A Teen-Age Breast Pump

Hooboy, am I tired of arty movie critics. You know, the ones who talk about Fellini and Rigatoni on National Public Radio, in low gaspy voices that sound like asthmatics on Quaaludes, so you'll know they're intellectuals and dreadfully earnest.

Me, I'm going to study real movies, for Americans: movies with grit and diesel fumes to them, and home fries, and application to everyday life. I mean the masterpieces that shaped this country: *Godzilla, Mothra, The Blob, Killer Shrews,* and *Rodan the Reptile Bat.* (Actually, I thought Rodan was a sculptor. Maybe he was a reptile bat too.)

Now, if you go to Europe, they will get arty on you. Like as not, they'll screen some grainy black-and-white atrocity about two tiresome people in love, and some reason why it won't work, and their sighs, and significant expressions, and soul-searching, and agonies, and eventual suicide. It will probably be based on an unnecessary novel by a French existential *philosophe.* You'll end up wishing you had never been born, and probably get drunk afterwards. The message will be that life is insecure, and unreliable, and sad sometimes, and doesn't make a grain of sense.

I bet you needed a French director to tell you that, didn't you? Only the Frogs would need a thousand years of intellectual posturing to learn what any C&W band knows at birth. Besides, if you want insecurity, *Godzilla* teaches that at any moment you can be stomped on by an enormous dinosaur. Maybe I'm just a country boy, but that seems like enough insecurity for everyday use.

If you want a movie up to the eyeballs in textured meaning (that's critic talk), watch *Killer Shrews*. It's real American Art — art you could sell at a NAPA outlet, forty-weight, with detergents and a discount if you buy it by the case. Great movie. See, there were a bunch of scientists on this island, maybe in the Fifties. They were experimenting with Radioactive Gunch or something. It's what scientists all do. They spilled it on some shrews.

Now, a shrew is about two inches long, and eats 27,000 times its weight in bugs every fifteen minutes. You can see that a big one would be a problem. Well, the Gunch made these shrews grow. Big shrews.

Trouble was, the movie had about a twenty-cent budget. The best they could do for giant shrews was to get collies and put shrew masks on them. (So help me. Watch it yourself.) You'd have an expendable character pursued through the woods by a herd of deadly shrews, all wagging their tails. There was no audio editing. Sometimes you could hear the shrews saying, "Woof woof."

Then there was *Jaws*. I didn't see it until last year, so maybe my experience with computer animation has prejudiced me. Everybody had told me about how terrifying the shark was and how they all had nightmares for weeks. (That's a good reason to pay seven dollars for a movie ticket.) To me, ol' Jaws looked like a rubber raft with teeth and a pole-axed stare, as if someone had put chloral hydrate in his last drink. And he ran into things, clunk. I was afraid the poor stiff might get blunted.

Artwise, though, I figure America hit a pinnacle in about 1957, when *The Blob* debuted, or debutted, or anyway came out. A meteor or space ship or something was zooming around the universe and crashed in Alabama, it looked like. Space aliens must have quality-control problems. They drop like flies, mostly near trailer parks in the South. Anyhow this one was full of slime. It jumped onto your hand and then dissolved you, and got bigger: Slime writ large.

For most of the movie a nomadic skwudge (I think that's how you spell skwudge) of sociopathic jello oozed around ominously (note the alliteration: it's literary), dissolving people. You'd see some guy in a vulnerable position, maybe under a car working on it. The camera would cut to gelatinous evil, *urgle blurg, glop.* Then to the guy under the car. Then to urgle blurg. The tension became unbearable, closely paralleling the cinematography. In a thousand theaters girls clutched their boyfriends extra tight. Those guys still eat jello in gratitude.

By the second reel the Blob was well on its way to metabolizing small-town America. One night it was eating Joe's Diner. Someone discovered that it didn't like being sprayed with fire extinguishers. (How smart was that? Who does like it?) It seemed that cold was the soft underbelly of intergalactic slime. Fortunately Joe's was in the only town in the country in which everyone had three fire extinguishers. They all came out and extinguished at it, and it chilled to death.

Then the movie ended. Good thing, too. It gets warm in the South, come morning.

There was a movie called *I Was A Teen-Age Werewolf,* but I never got to see it. In fact, there was a whole slew of movies about teen-agers who turned into various disagreeable things, a distinctly minor metamorphosis. In fact, teenagers being what they are, most parents wouldn't have noticed the advent of a werewolf. (I was inspired later in high school to write an autobiographical screen-play called I Was A Teen-Age Breast Pump, but I had to abandon the idea due to a shortage of material.)

However, the apotheosis of nuanced paradigmantic fin de siecle in the genre of le filme atrocieuse (Is that critic talk, or what? I made it up.)

was *Godzilla*. He was a bedraggled tyrannosaur, displaying signs of autism, who repeatedly came from the sea, breathing fire, and ate Tokyo. You could set your watch by it: Every Saturday afternoon at the Glebe theater, chomp, chomp, chomp. Godzilla was an allegory of unreached potential. He could have gone to a shipyard and worked respectably as a welding torch, but, no, he had to eat the city. Here we have a literary subtext on the repudiation of conventionality and society's inevitable punishment of the rebel. (He got chased into the sea where earnest-looking scientists dissolved him with oxygen bombs.)

Millions of kids, throwing popcorn boxes in Saturday matinees across America, learned from Godzilla lessons about the inexorability of fate, and about insecurity (at least in Tokyo)—not to mention how to sail a popcorn box for maximum range.

If that ain't Art, I don't know what is.

34

Oprah, Sensitivity, and Ready-Mixed Concrete

Tell you what, I've had it with whiners. Further, if I hear the phrase "self-esteem" again, I'm going to kill something.

It'll happen. Just wait. Some New Age, psychotherapeutically babbling little parsnip is going to gurgle to me about how arduous his life is, when he probably doesn't have a life to begin with, and about how it's somebody else's fault, probably mine, and his self-esteem is all bruised and rancid and has warts on it. And I'm going to stuff him into a concrete mixer.

No, wait. I've got a better idea. I'll pack him off instead to Marine Corps boot camp at Parris Island, in the festering mosquito swamps of South Carolina. I spent a summer there long ago, in a philosophy battalion. All battalions at PI were philosophy battalions.

The chief philosopher was named Sergeant Cobb, and he was rough as one. His philosophy was that at oh-dark-thirty we should leap up like spring-loaded jackrabbits when he threw the lid of a GI can down the squad bay. Then, he figured, we should spend the day at a dead run, except when we were learning such socially useful behavior as shooting someone at five hundred yards. He didn't care whether we wanted to do these things. He didn't care whether we could do them. We were going to do them. And we did.

The drill instructors had a sideline in therapy. They did attitude adjustment. If the urge to whine overcame any of us, Sergeant Cobb took his attitude tool—it was a size-twelve boot on the end of his right leg—and made the necessary adjustments. It was wonderful therapy. It put us in touch with our feelings. We felt like not whining any more.

I kid about it, but it really was philosophy. We learned that there are things you have to do. We learned that we could generally do them. We also learned, if we didn't already know, that whimpering is humiliating. The Marine view of life, which would eradicate American politics in about three seconds if widely applied, was simple: Solve your problems, live with them, or have the grace to shut up about them.

Can you imagine what this would do to the talk-show racket?

Fat housewife to Oprah: "My...I just won't...being so...heavy hurts my self-esteem."

Oprah: "So stop your damn sniveling and eat less. Next."

The Corps believed in personal responsibility. If your life had turned to a landfill, it might be somebody else's fault. Maybe existence had dropped the green weeny on your plate. It happens. But the odds were that you had contributed to your own problems. Anyway, everybody gets a raw deal sometime. Life isn't a honeymoon in the Catskills. Deal with it.

I remember a coffee mug in an armored company's day room: "To err is human, to forgive, divine. Neither of which is Marine Corps policy." There's something to be said for it.

Nowadays everybody's a self-absorbed victim, and self-respect and strength of character have become symptoms of emotional insufficiency. Oh, alas, alack, sniffle, eeek, squeak, the world's picking on me because I'm black, brown, ethnic, fat, female, funny-looking, dysfunctional, datfunctional, don't use deodorant, or can't get dates.

And sensitive? Dear god. If people suffer the tiniest slight, they call for a support group and three lawyers. (Support groups. When I'm dictator, we'll use'm for bowling pins.)

Whatever happened to grown-ups?

It's incredible the things people whinny about. Go to the self-pity section of your bookstore. It's usually called "Self Help." You'll find books with names like, "*The Agony of Hangnails: A Survivor's Guide.*" They will explain coping strategies, and assure you that you are still a Good Person, shredding digits and all. Other books will tell you that because you had an unhappy childhood (who didn't?) you are now an abused, pallid, squashed little larva, and no end pathetic. Other books will tell you how not to be toxic to your Inner Child. (I'm writing a book now: "*Dropping Your Inner Child Down A Well.*") We'd be better off if most people's inner children were orphans.

I once sat in on somebody else's group-therapy session, which was concerned about the morbid condition of the patients' self-esteem. I didn't understand the rules of therapy, and said approximately, "Look, maybe if you folks stopped feeling sorry for yourselves and got a life, things might be better."

I thought I was contributing an insight, but it turned out to be the wrong answer. The therapist, an earnest lady—all therapists seem to be earnest ladies—told me firmly, and with much disappointment in me, that this was No Laughing Matter. The patients' self-esteems were undergoing cardiopulmonary resuscitation, and I was suggesting that they get a life instead of picking at their psychic scabs. She reckoned I was pretty terrible.

Stuff'em into a concrete mixer, I say.

35

Women In Combat

Let's look bluntly (I'm not sure how you look bluntly, but I'm going to have at it) at whether women should be permitted in ground combat. And then I will make a splendid and fair-minded proposal, which will be applauded by radical feminists everywhere. My guess is that I'll be awarded life membership in the National Organization for Women.

Should women be in ground combat? Good lord no. Females have no place in the infantry, artillery, or armor. They are too weak, too delicate, and too small. They fade after about a day of heavy marching and lifting. They just get in the way. They will get men killed. The idea is bad, everyone who has been in the military understands it, but no one has the moxie to tell feminists, "No."

Maybe you haven't been afoot in a war zone. I have. In the mid-Sixties I was in armor in Vietnam with the Marine Corps, spent a fair amount of time carrying a rifle, went through infantry training in Camp Geiger, which you don't want to try unless you are one healthy young buck. Let me tell you some things about ground life in war zones.

It's brutally physical. Try unloading a truck carrying mortar rounds. Hump sixty pounds uphill in Asian heat for an hour. When I was a Marine a flame-thrower weighed, if memory serves, seventy-five pounds. Try humping that sucker up hills of greasy North Carolina clay when you slide back almost as much as you go forward and your lungs are burning till you can hardly breathe. Try breaking track on armor when a platoon in trouble needs fire support right now. Don't talk about it. Don't theorize. Try it. In Lejeune we force-marched day after day, on three and a half hours sleep. No, that's not exaggeration. Try it.

OK. Go to your local gym. If you aren't a member, pay the ten bucks for a day pass, and watch. Stand around for a couple of hours, and watch what men lift. Watch what women lift. See whether you can detect a pattern.

Women don't lift slightly less than men, and aren't slightly weaker. They lift enormously less. They are catastrophically weaker.

Don't take my word. Go. Look.

I'm 53, five-feet-ten, 180, in better shape than average for my size and age, but nothing spectacular. I never amounted to much as an athlete. I go to the gym to stay strong enough to carry my scuba tanks. If I walked into a Marine gym and said I was the strongest guy there, the Corps would have to be disbanded, because you can't fight while uncontrollably laughing.

But I'm far and away the strongest woman I've seen at Gold's in ten years of membership.

For example, I do fifteen sloppy reps on the bench machine with 270, and fifteen reps with 200 on the lat pull-down machine (the chin-up machine, if you will). It's respectable. That's all it is. There are guys there who could lift that much with me sitting on top of it.

I've never seen a woman bench more than eighty (which is real rare, but not even warm-up weight for a man). I don't think I've ever seen a woman pull eighty on the lat machine. Twenty to forty is normal for them.

Don't call me sexist. Don't tell me I'm trying to be "macho." (Or do. I don't care.) Go look.

Want documentation? There is a branch of research called exercise physiology, which has studied the physical capacities of men and women in near-infinite detail (largely to help in training athletes.) Check relative cardiac capacity, erythrocyte counts, muscle-mass-to-body-mass. I'm not making wild assertions. You can find all of this in any university library.

Now, what do these physical differences mean for society outside of the military? Almost nothing. A woman doesn't need strength to be a surgeon, professor, senator, journalist, or CEO. But weak women will get men killed in war. I've seen wars. I've been on casualty wards. So have a lot of men. For us, war isn't abstract, and getting men killed to appease feminists isn't cute.

I promised to make a splendid proposal. Here it is. Let's take 100 males just out of basic training, and 100 females, chosen at random. Let's take them all to Camp Lejeune, North Carolina, in a rainy October. We'll put sixty-pound packs on them, give them rifles and a full load-out of ammo.

Then we'll force-march them, at a fast pace set by an infantry sergeant, until they drop. I mean literally drop: can't stand up any longer. No stress time-outs, no little green cards to wave, no trucks to carry their gear, no slowing down. Hump till they crump.

This is what happens in combat: grim, unremitting physical effort with no sleep. Maybe it's humping with rifles and seven-eighty-two gear, maybe it's breaking track on a P-5, maybe it's unloading those miserable six-bys. It's physical.

If the women keep up, I'll shut up. If they keep up, all critics of putting women in the infantry will have to shut up.

Here is a wonderful opportunity for radical feminists everywhere. But know what? I'll get a lot of screeching and howling because of this column, accusing me of sexism and patriarchy. What I won't get is a call by feminists to make the test. They know what would happen.

36

The Confederate Flag

I believe that if I hear one more black politician hollering about how the United States is no damn good, and nobody in it is any damn good, and everyone discriminates against blacks, and denies them opportunity, and represses them, and doesn't do everything they want, and expects them to behave, I'm going to start bellowing.

It won't do any good. But I'll feel better.

Now, I don't want to associate promiscuously with facts, or state what we all know to be true. I'm a journalist, and I respect the traditions of my trade. But if I didn't, I think I might wonder why, if there is no opportunity in this country, everyone else has managed to flourish like kudzu on a Georgia road cut. No opportunity? A rock could succeed in America. Half the earth wants to come here because there's opportunity. Why do you think Mexicans swim the Rio Grande every night with their lives contained in plastic bags? ("Eet ees because we want to be repressed and have no opportunity.")

Gimme a break.

Remember the Jews on the Lower East Side of Manhattan in the Twenties? I guess they came because they were tired of all that opportunity in Poland. Anyway, they had it rough. The times were ugly and so was the place. There were fewer violins and more crime than is generally recognized now. They, and for that matter the Italians and Irish, didn't have the advantages blacks now have: the welfare, or subsidized housing, or free breakfasts for the kids, or Medicaid. Nor did they have a vast array of laws aimed at letting them advance regardless of merit. Most places wanted to keep Jews (and the Irish and Italians) out.

But they worked like sled dogs, went to school at night, saved pennies to put the oldest boy through school. Then he sent money back from the law practice and put the other kids through. It worked. People moved up. They did it the hard way, because that was the only way available, but they did it.

The opportunity was there, and they took it.

Opportunity has grown since then, grown mightily. Success has gotten steadily easier in America. In 1975 the Vietnamese appeared. The predictions were that they would go to the slums to be pickpockets and prostitutes. I guess their English wasn't too good at first, so they didn't get the word. They went to the suburbs instead and started restaurants.

The closest they got to sweatshops was McDonald's which, by world standards in sweatshops, is pretty lame. Soon they were spitting out valedictorians and showing up in droves in the better universities. (You've heard the joke about Asian SATs? Yeah, 800 math and 200 verbal.)

One year, so help me, a Viet kid was valedictorian at the Naval Academy. That's discrimination, no doubt about it. What better way to oppress a kid than to give him a free education and command of an aircraft carrier? I do it all the time.

We're a racist country? U. Cal Berkeley is 70% Asian. The United States is 2% Asian. Man, ain't that some ineffectual, didn't-work, pathetic, just plain *sorry-ass* discrimination? I could discriminate better than that, any morning before breakfast, and I'm from West Virginia.

Why do the Viets succeed? Because they are smart, courteous, ambitious, studious, and have a work ethic that would frighten Calvin. Their parents tell them to come home with As or don't come home. They never miss supper.

Last year I went to a favorite restaurant in Little Saigon, here in the Virginia suburbs of Washington. When it opened in the mid-Seventies, the kids in the family waited tables, keeping labor costs down, and the parents cooked. Some of the same kids, now women, still wait tables. I asked one of them what she did in the daytime.

"I'm an electrical engineer," she said. "I do wide-area networks."

Oh.

I reckon if we racist Americans tried to oppress her, it didn't work.

How about the Hispanic hordes? They aren't doing as well as did the Vietnamese. Nonetheless, I notice Hispanic restaurants popping up everywhere, like ticks on a hound dog. Hereabouts, Hispanics have taken over the market for unskilled labor. Why? Because if you work hard, show up, and do a good job, people hire you. (The foregoing is a blinding insight. Copyright: me. Patent applied for.) The young ones speak Standard English after a few years in the US, not Hisbonics after two centuries. They're rising.

I have to wonder where the dearth of opportunity hides. I can't find it.

Blacks today have advantages that would have turned the Irish and Italian immigrants bright purple with envy. Education is compulsory. Libraries abound. Welfare provides a breathing space for study. Blacks get affirmative action in just about everything. If American universities bent farther over backwards to accommodate blacks who didn't measure up, much less any who might, they'd be limbo dancers.

Are we Americans the cause of the ills of blacks? Think about this: In Washington we have a black mayor, a predominantly black city council, school board, teachers, parents, and students, and a very high per-pupil budget. (Now, when I want to discriminate against people, my first step is to give them political control of the national capital. Isn't that how you do it?) Oh, the heart-rending unfairness of it all. My soul curdles.

The schools are among the worst in the nation.

Oppression? Check to see what blacks need to get into universities, and what whites need. Oh yeah, we're discriminating out the gills. The United States regularly lowers its standards for blacks, offers special programs, recruits blacks who don't come close to qualifications required of whites, does everything but kidnap them and stuff them bodily into classrooms and jobs. Ask what proportion of black officers in the military would get in without special waivers.

If that's discrimination, I could use some of it.

Blacks, sez me, don't suffer from a lack of opportunity, but from an unwillingness, or inability, to take advantage of it. If the Vietnamese can rise from rice farmer to electrical engineer in a generation, then so can anyone who has the brains and chooses to work. And if they don't rise, I figure they didn't have what it takes. This country is awash in opportunity. Fish or cut bait.

37

Zoology in A Country Kitchen

We have voles. At least, we had a vole — or it may be that a vole had us. It is hard to tell with voles. The having and the had are separated, in the case of voles, by a point of view only.

The weather was frosty the other morning. The fire had died overnight in the stove, so I stumbled into the kitchen to start coffee, without which life is impossible in the Reed household. As I reached into the sink to fill the pot, a portion of the sponge turned black, skittered to a corner, and then hid beneath the stopper. Readers may doubt this, but I assure them that I saw it happen.

The transformation of sponges awakens my natural interest in poltergeists and fairies. I have always believed, or at least hoped, that things in kitchens might turn into interesting creatures — teapots into small dragons that would hiss in corners but get out of the way of the broom.

Anyway, the little fellow was the size of a mouse who had been on short rations. He had only the barest points of eyes, suggesting that the places he liked best were all underground, and had the longest, twitchiest pink snout, which he poked from beneath the stopper in frantic investigation. His tail was an embarrassment — stubby and rather accidental-looking arrangement, such as one would leave at home on a

Sunday walk. The beastling was shivering horribly because there was a half-inch of water in the sink and he had been unable to get out. One would expect an animal born of sponge to do rather well in water, but in fact he didn't.

I scooped him into a quart jar by way of rescue, and discovered that the scooping raised a question I hadn't fully anticipated. What does one do with a quart jar of madly scrambling — what? Clearly not a mouse, not a rat, not a mole—the forefeet were too small — not anything else of which I knew.

We decided that he was a vole, or at least that he would henceforth be a vole. To this end, we avoided looking in the dictionary so as not to be disappointed. My wife suggested that, rather than stand there forever in the manner of a zoological park, I should put him in a large clay casserole. We did, adding shredded newspaper for him to hide under and dry out in. (I know "dry out in" will offend the linguistically fastidious, but in times of crisis prepositions must fend for themselves.) I added a dog biscuit. Shortly an energetic crunching issued from the casserole. With voles, it seemed, mere panic does not get in the way of eating.

The acquiring of a foundling vole involves rather more than simple removal from the sink. Small animals are not evanescent. They last. One must do something with them. What? Throwing a scurrying furry animalcule into the snow to freeze was not something we were going to do. On the other hand, letting him go in the house did not seem the best thing. He might eat books. He might make more voles. He would almost certainly make more voles. My wife set forth to buy a cage.

Meanwhile, I dug beneath the snow for leaf mold, warmed it, and put it in the casserole. Our charge disappeared beneath it with much squeaking and crunched industriously on his dog biscuit. A sheet of quarter-inch screen weighted with a brass frog seemed to ensure his continued presence. Seemings are much to be watched.

My wife returned with an over-priced, uptown, chromed cage with an exercise wheel. It was the sterile sort of cage that would attract a vole accustomed to a high-rise with an elevator. Homey cages are not to be had nowadays. I spent an hour assembling it according to inscrutable instructions, during which I invented several new kinds of cages—cages with flaps pointing in unusual directions, cages with double walls and no roof.

Alas, our vole had left the casserole. How he did it is a mystery, although an animal that began as a sponge can doubtless do many surprising things. We sometimes see him rushing along the baseboards, attending to various errands. One such errand is the removal of beans from a stuffed duck, followed by their storage in the pocket of my armchair. Maybe he means it as a token of friendship. I suppose we will invest in a live trap to get some use out of the cage. Meanwhile, we have our vole, and he has us.

38

The South: An Unapologetic Remembrance

God, I weary of the huffing and puffing against Southerners. I know, you have to forgive a lot in Yankees. They don't know any better. I understand. But I do get tired of the unworthy telling me what a terrible place the South is.

I'm not sure how to explain the affection the South inspires in those who were raised there. Maybe it can't be explained. To me, the South meant slow hot barefoot summers in the small-town Alabama of the mid-Fifties, when I roamed the wooded outskirts with a BB gun and learned the mysteries of Kentucky windage from the coppery flight of a BB. The South meant afternoons on the rusting foot bridge over the swampy lowlands near the Valley Gin Company, shooting for happy solitudinous hours at mosquito hawks ("dragon flies" to the unknowing).

To this day I can see those iridescent blue bugs perch on glowing green foliage, hear the flitter of transparent wings.

The South to me was gorgeous speech with rounded edges, a green unhurried land, an easy friendliness encountered in ramshackle frame stores that sold peach soda and Moon Pies and shotgun shells. The friendliness was not lack of character. These people could get real hard if you leaned on them. But I liked that too.

And there was a luscious sensuality that hung in the air, that pervaded life. Men were men and women were women. It beat hell out of unisex.

On the town square of Athens, Alabama stood the Limestone Drug Store, run by a profoundly Southern, rumpled, red-haired old man in his seventies named, I eventually learned, Mr. Chandler. To the boys of Limestone County, he was just Coochie. Coochie liked children.

In his narrow store, next to the soda fountain with a pimply soda jerk, were tables where the eleven-year-old tribe sat, BB guns and ball gloves piled by the door. A rack of tattered comics, which no one ever bought, served as bait. Every afternoon when school was out, the assembled boyhood of Athens munched nickel pecan pies, drank lemon cokes, and hollered "Geeyaw!" and "Lookit!" while devouring volumes of Batman, Plastic Man, and the Green Lantern. It was wonderful.

Coochie, for whom I think the enterprise resembled bird-watching, sat behind the counter and smiled. He lost money on us. He didn't care. The Limestone wasn't some damn Northern chain run by accountants. It was his store.

This was the Southland as I saw it. Nowadays, whenever the South comes up in Washington's political discourse, it is consigned to eternal damnation for being mean to blacks. The implication always is that the North by contrast exhibits a positively cloying degree of racial solicitude. You could easily think that angels perched on lampposts along Pennsylvania Avenue, singing freedom songs.

Now, god forbid that I should be against hypocrisy, but a good thing can be carried too far. If I were black there would be some things in the South today, and more in its past, that I would not like. But I believe I would also reflect, were I black, on the racial harmony and togetherheid displayed in Anacostia, Bedford-Stuyvesant, Newark, South-Central LA, Boston the Fount of Kennedy's, and the far end of State

Street in Chicago, where the milk of interracial solicitude manifests itself in the warehousing of unwanted blacks in awful housing projects.

The South once espoused segregation, and said it did. The North today practices segregation, and says it doesn't. The moral difference is—what?

How could a city be more segregated than Washington? When do the most self-admiring liberals discover a yearning for the broad vistas of the Maryland suburbs? Why, just when the eldest child reaches school age. And what is the first thing racially correct parents ask about a school? The proportion of blacks to be found there.

Naw, ain't no discrimination in the North.

If I had to guess the real reason for the voguish hostility toward the South, I would ascribe it to cultural incorrectness. The South has always been intransigently itself. More than in any other region, people in those darkling Tennessee hollers and smoky-soft peanut fields of Alabama will, if they don't like you, tell you where the town limits lie, and suggest that you make a detailed investigation of their far side.

One thing the citadels of Northern vanity cannot stomach is unapologetic dismissal.

As for me, when some racial politician from Chicago or wherever starts whinnying about the flying of the Confederate flag in states that he can't spell, I'm inclined to tell him to take a hike.

39

Psychotherapists As Ducks

I've figured it out. We'll build a great long sliding board down a mountain in California, like a ski jump. Then we'll catch all the psychotherapists, and write "DUCK" on them in red paint. Then we'll grease them. Next we'll charge yuppie duck-hunters to sit at the bottom with shotguns, and slide those slippery suckers down.

Hell, a California yuppie can't tell a psychotherapist from a duck.

We've just got too many therapists. They're everywhere, like sin and head colds. Especially on those talk shows with ugly fat women talking about relationships. I saw a huge flat-faced one, who looked like a sheet of dry wall with eyes—I think it was Rosy O'Donnell—but anyway she had this therapist lady going on about something called Social Anxiety Disorder, or SAD. As best I could tell, it means being uncomfortable at parties.

Now, there's a medical condition.

Before we go any further I ought to say we've got too many disorders too: Borderline Personality Disorder, Avoidance Disorder, Relationship Disorder, Characterological Disorder, and Just-About-Everything Disorder. SAD also means Seasonal Affect Disorder. We've go so many disorders that they're piling up on the same abbreviations, like dry leaves on a fire hydrant. Seasonal Affect Disorder means that you get depressed in winter when it's cold and dark and the wind howls like a lost dog and slush gets in your shoes and freezes between your toes. I guess that's a pretty unusual time to get depressed.

Anyway, Social Anxiety disorder, said the therapist lady with worried solemnity, affected 20 million Americans, or 47 million, or some number. However, there was hope. All you had to do was to take a pill and—who *would* have thought it—see a therapist at $100 an hour.

It's pretty much a therapist lady's response to everything. Bored? Take a pill and give her $100 an hour. Can't find your car keys? You've got Can't-Find-Your-Car-Keys Disorder. Take a pill and....

Tell you what. Pick your own pill. And send me the $100. I promise I won't talk to you about your feelings. Direct deposit would be good.

Now, it didn't use to be that everything people did without exception was a personality disorder. No. Time was, people figured they were bored or lonely or didn't know what life was all about. But who did? It was just life. A guy might be as in love with himself as a peacock with a new Corvette, but he didn't have Narcissistic Personality Disorder. He was just egotistical and tiresome. How did everything get psychiatric?

Insurance.

Years back, there weren't any therapists. You only had psychiatrists, who treated seriously sick people and probably made them worse, or treated seriously bored rich ones and made lots of money. Psychiatrists were mostly seriously sick themselves, but they had intimidating beards, so they got away with it.

Then some astute grafter noticed that the mass market was in mildly unhappy people in the middle class who wanted to talk about themselves. Psychotherapy leapt into existence. It wasn't a healing discipline. It was a marketing strategy.

Problem was, suburban women weren't going to pay $100 an hour to talk about their feelings. They were perhaps mildly irrational, but they weren't crazy.

The trick was to get somebody else to pay the $100 for them.

As it happened, the insurance companies didn't mind doing it, since it increased the cash flow and they skimmed off their bit. However, they only paid for medical conditions, not the distempers and minor miseries of existence. The answer of the therapy racket was to medicalize life. Nobody was normal. Everyone was sick. All behavior was a symptom.

The key to this parlor trick was the DSM, the *Diagnostic and Statistical Manual*, sometimes known as the Loon Book. It came to list a vast number of peculiarities, angsts, and habits that suddenly became Disorders. If a therapist could dredge the symptoms of a Disorder from a patient, insurance money flowed. Bingo. Anything in the Loon Book was billable, so pretty soon everything was in it.

Therapy spread like kudzu on a Georgia road cut. New disorders popped up daily. Some of them were splendidly wacko. There was briefly a boom market in Multiple Personality Disorder, with books and movies and chat rooms on the Internet for sufferers. (Why? I figure if you've got MPD, you *are* a chat room.)

The other half of this financial thunderstorm was a pharmaceutical flowering. If Bored-With-Your-Job Disorder was a medical condition, there must be a medical treatment. Surgery seemed excessive. How about…yes!…a mind-altering drug! It was brilliant. Many of the earlier vic…patients had been through the Sixties, so the concept was familiar.

Sex differences erupted. A depressed man would knock back several bourbons and go look at motorcycles he would never buy. He might break things, throw a few people off a bridge, or machine-gun a kindergarten. Guy stuff. A woman wanted an answer that was approved by a parental figure, who would tell her that It Wasn't Her Fault. Which is the principal message of the therapy trade. Doctors, being ego-struck god-figures, were just the ticket.

Whole factories began spewing pills: Prozac, Zoloft, Welbutrin, Xanax, Depacote. It got hard to find an unmarried woman over forty who wasn't high on one of them.

The pharmaceutical companies saw yet broader vistas. The next step was compulsory disorders. Pretty soon, if you were a little boy, and not actually asleep on your desk, or dead, you had Attention Deficit Disorder, and they made you take Ritalin. (If you *were* asleep, you had narcolepsy, and they made you take Ritalin. If they caught you taking Ritalin without a prescription, you went to reform school. Social policy is endlessly fascinating.)

The question I worry about is: If everybody's crazy as bedbugs and disordered, and needs enough drugs to frighten a Grateful Dead concert—how come nobody noticed it before? Five thousand years of history, everybody was crazy, and nobody knew? Yes, yes: We've got Self-Loon Nonobservance Disorder. Take a pill and....

I don't know. I guess I'm just a redneck, and don't understand things like I ought to, except camshafts. Still, if a hunting pack of therapists had come up my holler, with a pill bottle and a credit-card machine, and wanted to talk to me about feelings, I'da shot'em. But then, I have Practical-Solution Disorder.

40

Rock Salt and Feminist Tarantulas

Maybe I'm just a country boy at heart, and lack sophistication, and don't see things the way I should. But when I watch one of those radical-feminist women heave onto a podium, like the forehaunches of an under-nourished giraffe but with more hair on her lip, and start hollering and carrying on about what slugs and bandits men are, I start thinking of the curative powers of a shotgun full of rock salt.

I recommend a 12-gauge duck gun.

It's the incivility of these feminist people that gets to me. Most of them seem to have the manners of a guard dog , but without the utility. (I know, I know, I'm going to get angry letters. From guard dogs.) For pure bile, you can't beat a radical feminist. The average specimen can turn out bad temper for hours on end, like lumber from a sawmill, and any of it sounds like all the rest. The following, which gives the flavor, is from Andrea Dworkin, who I gather is a sort of museum-piece siege howitzer for feminism.

It's pretty much how they all talk. Listen:

"Men use the night to erase us…The annihilation of a woman's personality, individuality, will, character, is prerequisite to male sexuality, and so the night is the sacred time of male sexual celebration, because it is dark and in the dark it is easier not to see: not to see who she is. Male sexuality, drunk on its intrinsic contempt for all life, but especially for women's lives, can run wild, hunt down random victims, use the dark for cover, find in the dark solace, sanctuary, cover."

I do?

How does a man respond to such a broadside? The prose could use some lubrication, of course, and maybe a new set of plug wires, but I'm talking about the content. My first impulse is to reassure the poor woman: "There, there, Andrea, you're safe, nights just don't get dark enough." My second impulse is to wonder just how much radical feminists know about male sexuality, and what book they read it in.

I like to picture myself on a Saturday-night date in high school, parking on a back road.

My date: "You're driving kind of funny. I reckon it was the beer."

Me: "Why, no, Sally. I'm drunk on my intrinsic contempt for all life."

Sally: "You're so silly. Come here."

Me: "Soon…soon. Do you mind staying here by yourself for a bit?"

Sally: "Huh?"

Me: "I need to, uh, you know, run wild for a few minutes. Hunt down a few random victims. Use the dark for cover. Guy stuff."

Sally: "You nuts or something?"

Me: "It's…night, Sally…the sacred time of male sexual celebration."

Sally: "You're gonna do it *out there?*"

OK, I understand that the radical feminist ladies are a few French fries short of a Happy Meal. They can't help themselves. What I can't figure is why more-or-less grown-up editors publish all this clucking and scratching as if it made sense. And I also don't understand how the rules got fixed so that a Dworkin can say anything at all about men and get away with it—but men can't say anything back.

Any loon feminist can accuse men of being rapists, killers, sadists, and Marines. These are pretty serious charges. A fellow could take exception to them. But if I say something comparatively innocuous in return, such as that I weary of being harried by a rat-pack of diesel-fired tarantulas who mostly look like Rin Tin Tin's littermates—why, they get mad. (Yes, I know, that was a three-animal zoological-automotive metaphor. Patent applied for.)

I figure if radical-feminist ladies can talk ugly about us, then we can talk ugly about them. And we're probably better at it, which they might bear in mind.

What I say is, if you have pool-hall manners, you ought to expect to play by pool-hall rules. Any guy who doesn't work for the *Washington Post* knows this. Go into the wrong bar, and somebody will likely hit you over the head with a pool cue. Nothing wrong with that. But the assailant will grant you the right, while questioning your ability, to smack him on the head with your cue. Symmetry. Reciprocity. Conservation of parity.

Not those feminist people. They want to swing cues. They don't want to get swung at. I say let's treat'em equal.

It'll happen. Some day before long I'll be talking about something sensible, like a '57 Chevy with Carter AFBs and a three-quarter Isky and 17 coats of hand-rubbed Orchard Mist lacquer that looks like Chinese emerald carving if they'd done it right. Sure enough, some dog-biscuit feminist is going to sniff, "Ah, yes, boys and their toys. Boys will be boys. Intrinsic contempt for...."

And I'm going to say, "Mercy, lady, mercy. Yes, we males are a sorry lot, sinners all, and neck deep in iniquity. The shame of it bores into my soul. Now you go stand in the middle of Dupont Circle at high noon, with a pair of seven-by-fifty binoculars, and look real carefully all around, and point to one thing, with a moving part, that was invented by a radical feminist."

Then I'll go for my duck gun.

41

A Dispatch From The Klan

The following is a letter recently found in the attic of a building in Arlington, Virginia, that once served as headquarters of the American Nazi Party. The author, though unknown to me, is clearly a racist of the vilest sort. We may profit by understanding the mind of such a man.

From: George Rockwell, Arlington, Virginia. May 6, 1955

To: James Braswell
Grand Klagon
Knights of the Invisible Empire
Ku Klux Klan

Dear Klagon Braswell,

In answer to your concern about preventing the rise of the Negro race after the disastrous Supreme Court decision of last year, I am somewhat more optimistic than you. I believe that, by judicious policy, we can, if not eliminate the problem of Negroes, at least control it indefinitely.

We cannot place hope in extermination or deportation of Negroes *en masse*, nor is there real hope of the reinstitution of slavery. The public mood will not now countenance such measures. We need rather a means of subjugating the Negro race while appearing to have other ends in mind. Fortunately, I believe that it can be done. Permit me to suggest a plan.

First, the thorough demoralization of Negroes is essential. They must first be made dependent on Whites, and then persuaded that they cannot achieve anything of worth on their own.

I believe this end may best be accomplished by instituting an all-encompassing system of public welfare. As you know, many Negroes now live in a state of poverty. We must argue in Congress that decency requires the provision of federal payments to allow Negroes to live at a fit standard. The economy is growing at such a rate that the country can carry the burden without undue difficulty. We should stress the benefits for the children, as this invariably evokes a favorable response.

Once welfare has been instituted, I believe that it will come to be accepted as normal by Whites, and then forgotten. After Negroes have been for several generations dependent on the largesse of Whites, they will, having had no experience of self-sufficiency, lose all initiative.

However, welfare alone will prove ineffective. The next step will be to destroy all social structure among Negroes. The most we could hope for—dare we dream?—would be to frame the welfare laws in such a way that married Negro women could not receive aid. The result, if luck held, would be a sharp rise in bastardy. The women would not be able to raise their offspring well, and these in turn would produce further young out of wedlock.

We must strive to make universal illegitimacy seem a natural condition. Crime and further demoralization will assuredly follow.

The third essential step will be to ensure that Negroes receive as little education as possible, though of course we cannot phrase our intentions this way. Fortunately Negroes now have little tradition of academic endeavor. It may be hoped, and even expected, that if we provide them with poor schools, they will, having no experience of true education, not demand better.

Next, we must at all costs ensure that Negroes not learn Standard English. A Negro who speaks intelligible and grammatical English is likely to be accepted socially by Whites. The consequences would be incalculable. We must encourage the notion that the degraded English now spoken by Negroes is in fact a real language, to be conserved and cherished.

A grave problem is that there will inevitably arise among Negroes men of intelligence and determination who will endeavor to elevate the station of their people. These men will be very dangerous. We can better thwart them, not by opposition, which would harden their determination, but by inviting them into White society, feting them, and making much of them in the public prints. Vanity and privilege will emasculate them, while making other Negroes believe that their race commands esteem among the better classes of Whites.

In order to accomplish all of this, we must have the support of much of the public, and of influential institutions, particularly the press. I believe it is possible. We must argue, as noted above, that welfare is the road of compassion, and appeal endlessly to warm feelings unaccompanied by thought. The elites of the White world crave a sense of helping the downtrodden. They do not, however, want to make difficult decisions.

Those who question any of our program must be ruthlessly portrayed as being hard-hearted, motivated by cupidity, and filled with loathing of our African population. If we can somehow associate our opponents with Nazis, we will succeed so much the better.

The withholding of education is crucial. We cannot of course argue that Negroes need or deserve poor schools. However, the privileged of the nation transparently believe that Negroes are inferior to the other races, but do not have the self-awareness to see that they believe it. They will fall easy prey to reasoning that avoids placing any expectations on Negroes other than those of continued helplessness. We must provide the privileged with excuses for doing this.

For example, we should argue that requiring Negro students to learn grammar and mathematics constitutes a racially arrogant imposition of European culture. Because pampered Whites do not think Negroes able to succeed, they will, given any excuse at all, favor the lowering of standards in Negro schools. They will then censor any who point to failure and thus, by hiding it, ensure its perpetuation.

Finally we need to engender among the well-off and the press a visceral intolerance of any policies toward Negroes other than ours. Our current Senator from Wisconsin has shown how to do it. The attitude we need to inculcate among reporters, who fortunately are not very intelligent, is that if you don't agree with means to a high-sounding end, then you disagree with the high-sounding end. Intolerance fortified by righteousness is invincible.

You may find this an excessively optimistic program. No. If we can carry it off, I say to you that in the year 2000 Negroes will be concentrated in urban ghettoes, speak English barely comprehensible to Whites, live in shameless bastardy, and be so devoid of both schooling and self-respect as to be without hope of advancement.

Trust me. All things are possible with enlightened social policy.

Yours in hope,
George

OK, OK, Rockwell didn't write this. But…how would you know?

42

Rollin' The Pluke Bucket

You gotta understand about the Pluke Bucket and me in rural King George County, Virginia, in 1963. Maybe you didn't know you had to understand this. Well, you do. Life is full of surprises.

The county was then mostly woods, the high-school boys gangly farm kids who fished and hunted or pumped gas on long lonely summer evenings on Route 301. Towns ran from small to barely existent, and lay far apart. The only way to get anywhere, geographically or romantically, was by car.

By the time a he-child reached fourteen, he could name any car ever made, and some that hadn't been, by looking at three inches of tail fin. Then he hit fifteen, his skin turned to pizza, and he began to look at girls with shocked reappraisal. Whereupon he bought some smoking, oozing, cantankerous rattletrap of a jalopy that sounded like a tubercular's last minutes—and fell in love.

It is a biological fact that a boy can love a car. He learns its every quirk, the whirring of unlubricated speedometer cables, the tick-tick-tick of sticking lifters, the dying sough of the transmission. A car—*his* car—is security in the great dark world after the sun goes down, warmth in winter, status symbol, bar, codpiece, love nest, identity, and heraldic emblem. In all his life he may find no greater intimacy.

It was a big feeling to set out at night into those winding wooded roads, alone, skirting adulthood, feeling independent and, however prematurely, manly. My own courser, the Pluke Bucket, was a '53 Chevy that ran on three cylinders, when it got to three, had no compression at all, and handled in a curve like a wet bar of soap.

I didn't care. The Bucket was mine. I had for that wheel-borne tragedy the affection someone sensible might have for a faithful dog. ("Pluke" was a local coinage meaning roughly "poontang." "Gittin' any plukin'?" meant, "Have you had the amorous success attributed to French rakes with the cheerleading squad serially?" The truthful answer invariably was "no." It was an answer we didn't much use.)

By age fifteen, a stripling could talk for an hour without saying a thing his mother could understand. Most of what he said consisted of a laundry list of mechanical properties having totemic import for those gripped by car lust.

"*Ba-a-ad* fitty-sedden Merc, dual quads, bored and stroked, 3/4 Isky, phone-flow, magneto ignition, 3.51 rear, Positraction, glass packs. Goose 'at sucker, *Sceeech!* Udden udden udden."

Decrypted, this meant that the speaker had seen, or hadn't seen and was lying about, a '57 Mercury with modifications that would cause the motor to make loud noises and then probably explode. We didn't have the money to build genuinely fast cars. But we could dream.

The terminology wasn't without meaning, and embodied the male passion for controllable complexity. For example, "phone-flow" meant that the car in question had four gears, mediated by a shifter on the floor boards, as distinct from threena-tree (three on the tree), signifying three gears with the lever on the steering column. Phone-flow was better, especially a narrow-gate short-throw Hurst, especially for power shifting, udden udden, *blap! sceech....*

Just as knights recognized each other by colorful hooha on their shields, so we knew each other by our cars. It was talismanic and tribal. Our moms wouldn't have noticed if they had passed a flying fire truck, but we, in that instant of passing on a winding night road, instantly recognized each other—Charles with the fitty-sedden Chev 283, Butch in the fitty-three Ford with the bad lifters, Floyd in the unspeakably glorious '63 Ford 396 Police Interceptor. (He had graduated, and was making big money in a gas station.)

Most of us labored under the delusion that we were racing drivers. I remember having the curious idea that 75 miles an hour was a reasonable driving speed for all occasions. (I know, I know. Teenage boys are dumber than mud walls. If you had taken the aggregate brains of all the boys in King George County, and put them in a garden slug, that slug would have been under-powered.) Reflexes, God, and low traffic kept us alive.

Thing is, hormones don't take no for an answer. One night I was out driving, just driving, putting gas through the engine, feeling that wild male rush to do something stupid and defiant. In a reasonable age, fellows of fifteen would have been dismembering brontosauruses, or banging on each other with funny-looking axes, or putting cities to the sword. Guy stuff. My family didn't have much money. I couldn't afford a sword, or a brontosaurus.

So I started fantasizing that I was Stirling Moss, then a Formula One racing champion. This was late one night on Indian Town Road, a narrow lane shaped like a convulsing python.

The wind poured through the windows like a current of water. Frogs creaked in the swamp and bugs keened in the trees. It's tough being a bug: You screech in a tree all night, trying to get laid, and then freeze to death. It's kind of how teenagers look at life. I came toward a tight downhill unbanked S-turn that would have frightened an Alpine goat. I remember thinking, "Only Stirling and I can take this turn at seventy."

I had overestimated by one.

I remember lying on my back, miraculously unhurt, looking up at the gas pedal. The Pluke Bucket was neatly on her top in the ditch.

Being a practiced teenager, I began rehearsing how to explain it to my father. Space aliens put grease on the turn? Bandits stole the Bucket and rolled her while I pursued on foot? Gravitational anomaly?

Somehow, a week later, I was back on the roads, still dreaming of hot cams and log manifolds, of the smell of gasoline and brake fluid and supercharged big-bores screaming toward high revs, and the quick, sharp speed shift that I couldn't actually do but craved as a protest against the unsatisfactory nature of existence.

It was meaning. I still haven't done better.

43

Breeding Like Trailer-Park Amoebas

I'm trying to understand this Single Mom thing.

I'm not having much luck.

From time to time I watch the talk shows on the lobotomy box, mostly to depress myself and see how much strength of character I have. It takes strength, let me tell you. Not infrequently I find Oprah, looking like a beached whale balanced on her hind flippers, spouting about some sordid guest, whom she introduces as a Single Mom. Or it may be Jerry Springer, who is a sort of female Oprah, with his characteristic array of human mollusks. But they're all the same, celebrating reproductive incontinence among the lower orders.

"And here is LaSheryl, a *Sin-gle Mo-o-mmmm*! from Tuscaloosa who will share with us her struggle with the DeadBeat Dad...."

Always there is a cheery sound to this Single-Mommery. The tone is one of chirpy commendation. We immediately realize that LaSheryl is not to be understood as a culpable and gelatinous loser from the bottom muck of society, but rather as a symbol of courage in adversity, a brave and noble woman Doing Her Best, though maybe she needs counseling, as almost everybody does, and Oprah just happens to have a psychologist handy....

Huh? I thought courage meant people like Helen Keller, Amelia Earhart, Joan of Arc, or Margaret Thatcher. Nope, guess not. Courage, it seems, is a gal who looks as if she had wandered off from the set for Biker Babes, and has no virtues other than a functioning reproductive system and the frame of mind of a lending library. She is courageously going to let society give her money and look after her kids. Usually she has in her eyes the look of alert intelligence I associate with flat tires. She is combatively complacent about having brought forth a Dadless tyke. She invariably lives on welfare.

Which means on me and you.

And this puzzles me. I find myself wanting to say, "Woman, you don't pay to raise my kids. Why should I pay to raise yours? What are you, a brood mare?"

Am I missing something?

Of course, you can't say such things. Ain't politically correct. If you do suggest that maybe these women ought to get their tubes tied, then you get told that you are just no end uncompassionate and don't have any sensitivity.

Well, OK. I'm just a country boy, and don't understand advanced thinking. But I gotta wonder, when LaTanya and LaSheryl and LaRhombohedron are spitting babies out like M&Ms for the Halloween rush, three per Single Mom by twenty-seven fathers, one of whose names they remember—or anyway what he looked like—I have to wonder about their sensitivity too.

Fact is, when kids are born to adolescent mothers with no jobs, no husbands, no education, no idea what responsibility is or how to spell it, and no maturity, those kids are going to end up on the streets selling dope. That's a fact. They grow up miserable.

I've watched this mess with black Single Moms downtown, virtually the only kind they have downtown, and with shiny white mothers of sixteen in the shiny white suburbs of Washington. As a philosopher in West Virginia once said, "Hit don't work." They push their strollers along, like kids playing house but just too young, leaning hard on mom to baby-sit while they try to go to high school, not able to date, not ready to be mothers, trying a job that's too big for them with no help, not bad but just not ready.

Even when the mothers are older, and lots are, hit still don't work. Yes, a female executive from CBS with the default chip on her shoulder can hire enough day-care to pull it off, sort of, and that's a lot of why this atrocity continues: Chips under the feminist shoulder-pads. But it doesn't work at all for most.

The talk-show ladies say it's liberation. Where I come from, it's called child abuse. Sez me, the children ought to be given to decent parents, and the mothers ought to be put in jail.

Further, I think we all know that massive illegitimacy doesn't work. We just somehow don't have the moxie to say, "Stop."

I tell you, this country is nuttier than Aunt Sally's Christmas fruitcake, and you know how much rum she puts in that sucker. We go in for hysterias, obligatory moods, odd stampedes and lemming orthodoxies. Remember Prohibition? A pack of battleaxes with too much time on their hands decided that booze was a satanic plot, and the country went into contortions for more than a decade.

Then there was Joe McCarthy, and we went to bed for years looking underneath the bed for a Communist. Obviously if Communists were witless enough to sleep under beds, they couldn't have been much of a threat, but never mind. Then came the Sixties, the silliest damn thing ever to happen to an unsuspecting continent. I know. I helped it happen. None of these things made sense to Europeans who, though boring, aren't crazy. We are.

We're doing it again, only this time it's feminism. That's what's driving the Single Mom lobby—feminism, and the fear of saying anything blacks don't like, though sodden fatherlessness is spreading fast to whites. Once again we're racing en masse in directions that most of us know make no sense at all. Come on: How many of us really think that massive illegitimacy is a good idea?

Maybe someone needs to say it plainly: "Casual bastardy is immoral, contemptible, reprehensible, bad for children, bad for society, and ought to be stopped. Now." (Hmmm. I think I just did say it.) Sometimes there are reasons for conventional morality. The reason usually is that it works. Why is it that we permit a ratpack of congenitally dyspeptic diesel dikes to impose this on us?

I don't get it.

44

Marrying With Abandon

I reckon I'll marry my desk. It makes as much sense as anything else these days.

I got the idea after reading about how homosexuals wanted to marry each other. The idea didn't seem any sillier than, say, bathing in used motor oil. I don't have anything against homosexuals. On the other hand, I don't see why they should escape the suffering inflicted on the rest of us. After they tried marriage a little, I figured, they would be supporting a law to make it illegal again.

Thing is (I continued figuring), if we're going to reform marriage, we ought to do it up right. No half measures: Reform it until it hollers for mercy. I mean, if marriage isn't going to be tied to reproduction, or to common sense, why should it be restricted to couples?

If Joe Bob can marry Sally, or Willy Bill, why can't he marry both of'em? Call it heterohomogamy. (I'm manfully resisting an impulse to write about a bisexual built for two.) If two homosexuals have a constitutional right to marry, why don't three? Or three heterosexuals? Why not bigamy, trigamy, even fourgamy?

Actually, I can imagine the marriage of vast clusters of people, of whole phone books. You could marry your suburb. I think it's protected by the First Amendment's right to freedom of assembly.

I'm tired of being oppressed by the white male biarchy and its phallocentric anti-heterohomogamous hierarchical prejudices.

Yeah. Hooboy.

Why stop with marrying Scarsdale? The Supreme Court needs to look into the unconstitutional ban against marriage between species. Why can't Jim Bob marry his faithful dog Birdshot? (Actually, because if Birdshot got wind of it, he'd be off like a rocket. Dogs are faithful, but they're not crazy.)

The truth is that guys form bonds of affection with dogs that are almost as strong as those they form with a restored '58 Ford with monster four-barrel carburetors and three coats of hand-rubbed Kandy-Color Red metal-flake enamel. A man will throw a cat into a wood chipper and reckon he's made a contribution to society. He'll love a dog.

Granted, a fellow's relationship with a dog is in some respects unlike marriage. A dog usually likes you. The average pooch stays around until one of you croaks. Still, mutual affection isn't an absolute bar to matrimony.

What I want to know is: What right does the Supreme Court, nine funny-looking judicial nonentities in black nighties, have to tell me with whom I can plight my troth? (I wish I were a little more sure what a troth was. It sounds like something a horse might eat from. I want to marry my horse.)

Yes, I know. Conservatives, ever sloshing around in the rearguard of advanced thought, will object to a liberating conception of marriage. Phallocentric heterohomogamophobic biarchical males (or maybe I mean biphallic heterowhatever-I-said archocentric ones: It's hard to tell) will argue that matrimony with a pooch-dog is absurd. Who says?

In reality, inter-speciesist love has always flourished, especially in sheep country. (Incidentally, my spelling-checker thinks "speciesist" should be "spacesuit." See? Biased software.) Hushed reports circulate in New York of liaisons with chickens and even gerbils.

These affairs of the heart have been the subject of cruel humor. For example, after the Gulf War, American GIs asked, "What do you call an Iraqi with a sheep under each arm? (The answer was "A pimp." Is that insensitive, or what?) They also asked, "What do you call an Iraqi with a sheep under one arm and a goat under the other?" ("A bisexual.") These sick attempts at humor, like the frequent reference to camels as "war brides," underline a deep cultural discomfort with a more accepting view of marriage. At the same time, they show that a reactionary prejudice has begun to be questioned.

Isn't it a matter of individual freedom? If a man wants to marry a chicken, society has no business interfering in what at bottom is a matter of private conscience. Of course a trans-phylum marriage cannot be expected to result in children, but the loving couple could adopt. Many children now languish in orphanages, probably eating nothing but cold porridge, because there aren't enough heteropatriarchal couples who want to adopt.

Children today, raised in antiquated conservative beliefs, might laugh at a classmate whose mother clucked, or tried to nest in the supply closet. This intolerance can be remedied through progressive schooling. We have booklets today to counter homophobia, as for example, "Sally Has Two Daddies." How about, "Billy's Mommy Has Feathers"?

Teachers could explain that diversity is good. Sez me, the courts need to give forward-looking thought to one of the last remaining barriers to a truly enlightened view of marriage: Live-ism. By this I mean totally unjustifiable discrimination against the non-living. Why is it that I may not marry, say, an inflatable wife? Or man or sheep, of course.

The idea is not as curious as it may seem. Love between people and the inanimate is well known. Little girls clearly feel genuine affection for their dolls. Naval captains sink loyally, if not very intelligently, with their ships. Fighter pilots love their airplanes almost as much as they love themselves, with women a distant third. Why an unreasoning prejudice against silicone?

Entire silicone women are sold on the Internet for about five grand, not just piecemeal by Dow-Corning. They are less engaging than "real" women (though who are we to decide who is "real"?) On the other hand, they don't cluck, bleat, quack, or complain about the scuba gear in the middle of the floor. I've never heard of silicone men, perhaps because women aren't loony enough, but we could pass a federal law requiring their manufacture.

Again, other children would have to learn to be tolerant of nontraditional families based on plastic. A booklet would help: "Bobby's Mom Softens When it Gets Hot."

This column is getting out of hand. There's such a thing as too much social progress. I'm still going to marry my desk. Nice legs, four of them, but no knees. Y'all come.

45

Growing Up Dumber Than Anvils

Today: American schools and how they got to be the dark night of the mind—why our children's heads have become vast, hollow, echoing places, like empty oil drums, and why they can't read stop signs without counting on their fingers. After today, you'll never have to read about education again. You'll know everything. (I figure columns are like appendectomies. You only need one.)

Here it is:

Our kids can't read because we don't care whether they can read.

Yep. That's how simple it is. The problem isn't television or drugs or even invisible pervasive dumb-rays shot by space aliens. There's no mystery about it. We just don't care. We talk a good show, but it's all talk. If we were serious, we'd do something.

Which wouldn't be hard. There are problems we can't solve, like AIDS, and problems we won't solve. Education falls into the second category.

We know how to run good schools.

To teach, say, algebra to eighth-graders, get a smart teacher lady who knows algebra, and who likes adolescents, to the extent that is

possible to like adolescents. Find a solid workbook with lots of problems. Trap her, the workbooks, and the students in a room. Tell her to
teach—not just sort-of teach but to stretch the minds of the libidi-
nous little monsters, and tell her to give bunches of homework, and
that the school will support her if she flunks the nonfeasors, if it
means the entire class and all their relatives to remote generations and
strange phyla. Then go away.

This works. It always has. We just won't do it.

Thing is, parents have to help, and too many of them don't. They
aren't really interested, or they're swamped trying to be single mothers
or make the mortgage, or they both have jobs and want the government
to raise their children. This isn't good enough. Parents need to explain
to their churning hormone-wads that learning is not optional. And
there have to be consequences.

Fathers in particular should speak as follows to their treasured exper-
iments in homebrew DNA-splicing:

"Son, I don't give a faint, wan, bleary-eyed damn about your dumb-
ass self-esteem. I've been forty-eight years on this sorry planet, and
nothing has ever struck me as quite so uninteresting as your self-con-
cept. All I care about is algebra. Here's an equation. No algebra equals
no Saturday night dates."

If this sounds brutal, good. There's nothing like the expectation of
dismemberment to boost performance. Remember, you aren't asking
the impossible of the tad. If he isn't smart enough to learn algebra, he
shouldn't be in the class. If he's smart enough, then he can blessed well
learn it.

Kids will get away with what they can get away with. But if young
Willy Bob realizes that you really will keep him in on Saturday night,
and some evil-minded football player will get his darling Sally Carol
with the lovely blue eyes and golden hair and nine-pound braces, and
park with her on deserted back roads, well, old Willy Bob will factor

quadratics something fierce. Quadratics will become an endangered species, and hide under rocks.

And I'll tell you something else. The kid will respect you for it and, eventually, respect himself. Kids esteem themselves when they have accomplished something worth esteeming. (That's a piercing insight. I may patent it.)

Granted, if people insist on performance, life won't be real easy for a few years. Teen-agers are intolerable. It's a design feature. Boys act like James Dean in a sulk. If you have a daughter, she will play your heartstrings like a bull fiddle, because girls do that, and then relapse into tyrannosaur mode and shriek. She'll tell you piteously that she'll do better, and her life will be ruined if she can't go to some concert of musical illiterates masquerading as a rock band. The answer is still, "No. I love you, but you are going to do your algebra. We are now through with this discussion."

The aforesaid works. It works better with some kids than with others, and you always lose a few, but it works better than anything else. Thing is, we aren't going to do it. The schools aren't going to improve. The teachers unions, obsessed with protecting their jobs, are absolutely in the saddle. With exceptions, but not enough exceptions, they don't like the whole idea of education, so they jaw-storm about feelings and attitudinal change and empowerment, whatever that is. We don't care enough to buck them.

Still, in moments of fatuous optimism, I reflect that it could be done. If a few hundred parents showed up at school, with a rope and a focused look, results might follow. In fact, when I'm dictator, I'm going to put a bounty on the National Education Association. Bag one and bring the varmint in stuffed, and you'll get a keg of Budweiser and three free nights of bowling. It would be like duck hunting, but more satisfying.

Next I'd pass some laws. To teach in grade school, you would have to be in the upper third of the GREs, and sign a statement that you hated self-esteem worse than rabies or pellagra, and that you would teach

167 of Fred Reed

children to read and write and know stuff and if you didn't you would be boiled into tallow and made into candles and sent to India, where they can't read at night.

Further, to teach in high school you would have to be in the top ten percent, and have a degree from a real university in the subject you taught. Not in education. You can't teach what you don't know. Then I'd raise salaries by five thousand dollars a year, each year, until I got bodacious fine teachers that you could show in the county fair.

You can catch anything with the right bait. It would be about as hard as getting ticks in a cow pasture. I reckon you might need a long afternoon to find twenty kerbillion smart women who wanted to actually contribute something to society, and get home when their kids did. I'd give'm great retirement programs and their summers completely off. Pretty soon they'd get respect from the community because they'd be worth respecting.

And you know something? It would do wonders for the kids' self-esteem. Who feels happier about himself—a child with a decent education and the confidence that goes with it, or one who barely speaks English, can't puzzle out warnings on a table saw, and figures to spend his life sleeping under bridges?

We could fix this mess. But we won't. We don't care enough. I reckon countries just plain get the schools they deserve. That's scary.

46

Sex, Mathematics, and Political Correctness

Many more men than women become lead engineers and theoretical physicists. Is the reason, as feminists assert, that society, the universities, and the mathematical professions discriminate against women? Or is the reason that men are naturally better at mathematics?

Those who believe discrimination to be the cause point out that the male mean (i.e., average) score on the math section of the Scholastic Aptitude Test is only slightly higher than the female mean—not enough higher, argue believers in discrimination, to account for the massive preponderance of men in jobs requiring high mathematical ability. The discrimination justifies affirmative action, goes the reasoning, in order to put equal numbers of women into mathematical jobs.

Maybe not.

The key is to understand that the average score does not in itself predict performance. The distribution is crucial. As an unrealistic example to illustrate the point, imagine a group of twenty women each of whom has an IQ of 100. The mean for the group will be 100. Now imagine a group of twenty men, ten of whom have IQs of zero, and ten of whom have IQs of 200. The average will again be 100—but the consequences will be very different. Half will be geniuses, and half will be idiots.

Look closely at the actual numbers. (They are from the research library of the Educational Testing Service in Princeton, NJ, which administers the SATs. The tests consist of math and verbal sections, with scores on each running from 200 to 800.)

From the 1983-84 testing period through 1988-89, (before the recent dumbing-down of the tests) the ratio of the absolute numbers of boys to girls scoring above 600 on the math section, a fairly high score, is 1.84 boys to girls, almost two to one. The ratio above 700, a quite high score, is 3.13 boys to girls. Above 750, which begins to be high indeed, 4.79 boys to girls. For scores of 800, there are 7.61 boys to girls. (The distribution is symmetrical: Men also predominate on the low wing of the distribution, which, along with greater aggressiveness, probably accounts for the roughly ten-to-one preponderance of males in prisons.)

From the very high scorers come the prominent engineers and research scientists. This goes a long way toward accounting for the predominance of men in the hard sciences. (On the verbal test, the differences are much smaller. For example in the same testing period there are 1.32 males per female with scores of 800.)

If the scores correlate with innate ability, and if the gap continues to widen with increasing ability, which in fact it does, then mathematicians on the order of Newton, Gauss, and Galois will almost always be male.

This distribution is well known in the testing community, and occurs across a wide range of tests. Because the reality is so politically incorrect, considerable effort goes into altering tests to disguise the difference, as for example the recent renorming of the SATs.

But, one might ask, do the scores measure real differences in ability? And how much of the difference is due to innate ability?

The SATs fairly obviously measure a mixture of intelligence and achievement. Separating the two isn't easy. People achieve more at things that interest them. Are boys more interested in mathematics, as they are in carburetors?

If the disparities between the sexes were slight, one might easily explain them as the result of such things as a culturally ingrained tendency for girls to take fewer math courses. Since more girls than boys take the test, one might suspect that their test population contains more students of low ability, which would bring down the female mean. (Here, however, the ratios are calculated using absolute numbers of scorers at given levels, obviating the objection.)

On the other hand, girls in high school study more and make better grades, which would favor the girls. In short, there is enough slop in the statistical gears to make doubtful any conclusions from small differences.

But the differences are not small. They are huge. What is the explanation?

Three possibilities come to mind. First, perhaps the tests are biased against females. If so, one must conclude that ETS, which is aware of the differences, deliberately designs its tests to keep women out of the mathematical professions. The idea is absurd. Second, perhaps secondary schools, even society as a whole, somehow fail to prepare extremely bright girls to compete against extremely bright boys, while preparing girls of ordinary ability about as well as boys of ordinary ability.

Well, maybe. If very bright girls for whatever reason take English courses instead of math (though when I was in high school, all college-bound students took the same courses), they presumably will do less well than boys who do take math. But then why do more boys than girls make 800s on the verbal test?

Third, perhaps men are just plain better at mathematical reasoning. If so, nothing can be done. This is the least politically correct explanation but it is also, I think, the one most in accord with the evidence.

If men are better mathematically, the implications for policy are substantial. In particular, quotas by sex cease to make sense. Firms, as for example defense contractors, should not be required to hire people who don't exist. If an engineering company refuses to hire a particular woman who is demonstrably the best qualified candidate, she has a legitimate complaint. If the company fails to ensure that half of its hires are women because it can't find qualified women, no one has a complaint.

This in turn implies that perhaps advancement should be awarded by ability, not by race, creed, color, sex, and national origin. Affirmative action—i.e., the enforced hiring of the unqualified—might almost make sense (but probably wouldn't) if native ability were equal. If ability isn't equal, the results will be high overhead, inefficiency, and incompetence for companies, and enormous resentment from the qualified who are passed over. And in the long run, it won't work.

Finally, perhaps it is time to rethink the hallmark tenet of today's compulsory political propriety, namely that all groups are in all ways equal. What if they aren't?

47

The Origins of Bushwah

Everyone and his pet goat has noticed that the media do a poor job of covering the news. The facts frequently aren't facts, the reporters conspicuously don't understand their subjects, and the spin is annoying. Why?

For lots of reasons. To begin with, newspapers necessarily attract certain types of people. To get the news, reporters have to be aggressive, willing to push their way over others and to ask questions people don't want to answer. They have to work well under the pressure. Because deadlines rule newsrooms, they often have no choice but to write superficial, half-understood stories. A reporter can't tell the editor, "Yeah, somebody *did* just nuke Capitol Hill, but I think we should wait to write about it until next week, when we have the facts."

Further, reporters have to submerge themselves daily in tedious details of unimportant stories about trivial people: Who wrote the check used to buy the fur coat that was obviously if not provably part of the bribe from the lobbyist of the trash-collectors' union to the mayor's wife? (Who really gives a damn?) Most reporting is neither interesting nor exciting.

It requires the soul of a CPA in a hurry, and reporters indeed amount to high-speed fact-accountants. The job quickly weeds out

those who don't want to be, who aren't comfortable with the compromises and pressure.

Human nature is such that some qualities do not often coexist with
others. For example, the aggressive and detail-minded are seldom studious or contemplative. Fact-accountants are not theorists. The cast of
mind of reporters is concrete, not abstract, their mental horizons short.
Reporters aren't stupid—most are quick and some are very bright
indeed—but they do not naturally look at the big picture. They do not,
for example, approach a new beat by reading books about it. Intellectual
they ain't.

To put it a bit too succinctly, the qualities needed to get the news pre-
clude an understanding of it.

Since most of the people in any newsroom fit this pattern, a culture
has evolved which supports the reporters in their natural inclinations. It
is a staple of reportorial philosophy that one does not have to know a
field to cover it. Any reporter, goes the thinking, should, given a week or
two to fill the Rolodex, be able to cover anything. Which in fact he can,
barely: Within a few days an experienced reporter can knock out copy
that usually is not ridiculously wrong. Neither is it very good. But that is
good enough.

A concrete example: A reporter assigned to the military beat and told
to cover, say, submarines, will pull everything he can find on submarines from Nexis and the morgue. He will learn who in the Pentagon
deals in submarines, who builds them, what the armed-services com-
mittees on the Hill think about submarines, whose districts profit from
the contracts.

He will not read books on the design of submarines, their history
and modes of employment. He will probably never quite learn what
they are for: plugging the GIUK Gap, for instance. Further, reporters
seem to be obligate technological illiterates: Our example will not learn
about phased arrays, convergence zones, the relation of the aperture of
a towed array to its angular resolution. He won't have the background

to understand such things even should he try. So he will go for politics, which he understands.

In short, he will learn everything about the politics and bureaucracy of submarines, and nothing about submarines.

The fundamental ignorance leaves him at the mercy of his sources. Since he will have no independent idea which of competing claims about a new submarine make sense, he will have to decide instead which sources seem to him more trustworthy. Seeming trustworthy is an art much studied in Washington.

Now consider the circumstances under which reporters work. Newspapers with few exceptions are understaffed. A computer magazine can have a writer specializing in CPUs and microcircuitry, another in software, a third in disk drives. By contrast a newspaper will have a reporter who covers Science-and-Technology.

The job is a bit like specializing in practically everything. It ain't doable. The field is too grand. It can be approximated by the very rare reporter with a strong technical bent and a lifetime of reading texts in biochemistry, vector analysis, neurology, and so on. These usually go to technical publications.

Back to our example, he of the submarines. His beat will be The Military. He can't cover it. The military is a vast, sprawling canvas of different services, weapons, missions, bases, much of it relying on exotic and highly disparate technologies. Further, it is all over the world. The reporter can't go all over the world.

So he will cover the Pentagon, which is convenient, and military politics, which he can believe he understands. They aren't the military. But they're convenient.

And here we come to a governing principle of newspaper journalism: Do what you have time to do. This is why you see stories reporting that some policy shop, say the National Coalition of Concerned Physicists (I think I made that up) says that we are all in danger from radioactive emissions from rutabagas. Maybe we are; maybe we aren't. The reporter doesn't have time or, perhaps, knowledge to find out.

To save labor, journalism has decided that the issuing of a report is in itself a story, not the beginning of one. The reporter therefore doesn't have to know enough to determine whether the report is correct. He merely has to announce its existence. The published account is inherently biased, even if the reporter covers himself by adding a one-sentence rejoinder from the rutabaga farmers. The important thing is that he gets a story easily, which is all he has time to do.

The policy shop understands all of this, and takes advantage of it.

Them's some realities of the news racket. We'll look at other from time to time.

48

Blacks And The Politics of Racial Extortion

Oh, Lord. I'd pull my hair out, if I had more.

On the Web I find that Henry Louis Gates Jr., the chairman of Afro-American Studies at Harvard, is demanding that whites pay reparations to blacks. It's because of slavery, see. He is joined in this endeavor by a gaggle of other professional blacks. I guess he'll send me a bill.

Huh?

I feel like saying, Let me get this straight, Hank. I'm slow. Be patient.

You want free money because of slavery, right? I don't blame you. I'd like free money too.

Tell you what. I believe in justice. I'll give you a million dollars for every slave I own, and another million for every year you were a slave. Fair enough? But tell me, how many slaves do you suppose I have? In round numbers, I mean. Say to the nearest dozen. And how long were you a slave?

Oh.

In other words, I owe you reparations for something that I didn't do and didn't happen to you. That makes sense. Like lug nuts on a birthday cake.

Personally, I think you owe me reparations for things you didn't do and never happened to me. I've never been coated in Dutch chocolate and thrown from the Eiffel Tower. I'll bet you've never done it to anyone.

I want reparations.

Kinda silly, isn't it?

But if we're going to talk about reparations, that's a street that runs in two directions. You want money from me for what some other whites did to some other blacks in another century. How about you guys paying whites reparations for current expenses caused by blacks? Not long ago blacks burned down half of Los Angeles, a city in my country. Cities are expensive, Hank. Build one sometime and you'll see what I mean. Whites had to pay taxes to repair Los Angeles for you. You can send me a check.

Now, yes, I know you burned LA because you didn't like the verdict in the trial of those police officers. Well, I didn't like the verdict in the Simpson trial. But I didn't burn my house and loot Korean grocers.

Over the years blacks have burned a lot of American cities: Newark, Detroit, Watts, on and on. Now add in the fantastic cost over the years of welfare in all its forms, of large police forces and jails and security systems in department stores. I can't live in the capital city of my own country because of crime committed by blacks. Toss in the cultural cost of lowering standards in everything for the benefit of blacks.

See what I mean?

Now, I'd view things differently if you said, "Fred, blacks can't get anywhere in a modern country without education. We know that. We need better schools, smarter teachers, harder courses, books with smaller pictures and bigger words. Can you help us?"

I'd say, "Hallelujah! Hoo-*ahh!* Not just yes, but *hell* yes. Let's sell an aircraft carrier and get these folks some real schools and get them into the economic mainstream." I'd say it partly because it would be the right thing to do, and partly because I'd like to add you guys to the tax base. The current custodial state is expensive. I'd just love for blacks to study and learn to compete and stop burning places.

But is it going to happen?

You may not believe it, but I, and most whites, don't like seeing blacks as miserable and screwed up as so many of them are. I spend a fair amount of time in the projects. Those places are ugly. It's no fun watching perfectly good kids turn into semi-literate dope dealers who barely speak English. It just plain ain't right.

But, Hank, what am I supposed to do about it? I can't do your children's homework. At some point, people have to do things for themselves, or they don't get done.

Maybe it's time.

I'll tell you what I see out in the world, Hank. I think blacks are too accustomed to getting anything they want by just demanding it. True, it has worked for over half a century. Get a few hundred people in the street, implicitly threaten to loot and burn, holler about slavery, and the Great White Cash Spigot turns on.

Thing is, whites don't much buy it any longer. Most recognize that what once was a civil-rights movement has become a shakedown game. Few people still feel responsible for the failings and inadequacies of blacks. Political correctness keeps the lid on—but everyone knows the score.

Which scares me, Hank. On one hand, blacks hate whites and incline toward looting and burning. (The whites you hate are the ones who marched in the civil-rights movement. Ever think about that?) On the other hand, whites quietly grow wearier and wearier of it. Not good.

On the third hand (allow me three hands, for rhetorical convenience) blacks keep demanding things. As I write, you demand reparations for slavery. Blacks in Oklahoma (I think it was) want money for some ancient race riot. Other blacks reject the Declaration of Independence, blacks in New York hint broadly at burning and looting over a trial, yet more demand the elimination of the Confederate flag, and the federal equal-opportunity apparatus, which means blacks, wants to sue Silicon Valley for not hiring nonexistent black engineers.

That's a lot of demanding for one month, Hank. What happens if whites ever say, "No"?

Now, how about you? You've got a cushy job up there at Harvard, and you can hoot and holler about what swine and bandits whites are. I guess it's lots of fun, and you get a salary for it. But don't you think you might do blacks more good if you told them to complain less and study more?

For example, if you want blacks to work in Silicon Gulch, the best approach might be to find some really smart black guys, and get them to study digital design, not Black Studies. That's how everybody else does it. It works. Then blacks wouldn't feel left out, and racial tension would decline. Sound like a plan?

Just out of curiosity, how many hours a week do professors of Afro-American Studies spend in the projects, encouraging poor black kids to study real subjects, Hank?

Oh.

49

Candy-Asses and Fern Bars

The papers nowadays sink beneath the weight of thought about the monument to the veterans of Vietnam, wondering whether it should be bigger, smaller, whiter, gaudier, or above water level. If I may speak for myself, I would just as soon not see a memorial built at all.

Other men who were in Asia in those strange, receding days may disagree, but I cannot see that the war is the proper concern of Washington. The city was never behind the veterans, neither the politicians who ran the war with the talent and morals of used-car salesmen, nor the crowds who ran through the street with North Vietnamese flags. No, here is not the place. There is impropriety in building a monument to the dead in a city that caused them to die, and wished them dead.

I propose that the city build a memorial to the Peloponnesian dead, or to those who fell at Sevastopol or Cannae. Washington at least was not the enemy of these. To rededicate Maya Lin's somber angle to men who will not have to see it is nothing more than decency. Living veterans ought not be honored by a tombstone.

If we must build a memorial to the veterans of Indochina, let us do it on Wake Island, where the refugees came in the last frantic exodus from Saigon. On Wake a monument would stand in the windy silence, under sunsets like the vast gorgeous radiances we saw in Asia, and not seem a part of any particular place or time. This would be fitting. A country that spurns its army in time of war should not commemorate them in time of peace.

If we must have a memorial in America, let us put it in a coal camp in a forgotten hollow in West Virginia, or in the smoky blue evening of some border town in Texas, or in the decay of the Bronx. From there came the men who fought the war. Don't erect it on the Mall to be psychically fondled by the literati, to be chattered over by hollow-chested little professors, the ghouls of the wars of others. The dead should not be displayed for voyeurs.

Besides, the sunken black wall is not a monument to the veterans. Already the chatterers have taken it from the men it stands for. The theoreticians of the art academies, knowing and caring nothing about soldiers, demand a funerary arch on its side to commemorate the sweating, literal-minded men who fought in the paddies. What have austere slabs to do with soldiers? I think back to my platoon at Parris Island, and wonder what Corporal Larry Reyes, a Chicano out of Fresno who died clearing a tunnel, would think of the dark wedge.

No, I don't wonder.

Those responsible never had it in them to design a monument to troops, and they didn't even try. What earthly sense does it make to allow an intellectual, Chinese, barely-adult artist to design a monument to fifty thousand grunts from Topeka and Amarillo?

I have no hard words for Maya Lin; may she flourish—but no one could have had less understanding of the men who fought the war. No, those who planned the black vee were thinking of themselves, not of soldiers—thinking of their little theories and what the professionals journals of art would say. I for one do not want to remember the Marines of 1967 by a memorial to the art department at Yale.

I have even heard it argued that the soldiers of the statue, if there is to be a statue, should be without rifles, as weapons might be controversial.

Here is bared the spirit of the thing: the chatterers do not want to memorialize the veterans as they were; they want to memorialize the veterans as they think they should have been. They want a monument to their political passions, a disarmed marble catechism in perpetual apology. The thing on the Mall really is Jane Fonda's wall. If I were among the dead I would not want my name on it.

If I were designing a memorial to my own taste, I would want an enormous bronze hand rising from the ground, making a rude gesture—no flag, no inscription, just a raised finger. Some might think it vulgar, but soldiers are vulgar. It would perfectly express my feelings about the war, the country, Washington, and the commission that designed Jane Fonda's wall.

*Written when a dispute was raging over the size, nature, and propriety of the monument on the Mall in Washington to veterans of Vietnam.

50

Whose Side Are Professional Blacks On?

Tell me, is there any functional difference between the average black leader and David Duke? Any difference, I mean, besides candor? Do they not produce the same practical results—i.e., precisely nothing good for blacks? Racists say straightforwardly that they think blacks are stupid and shiftless. The black leaders act exactly as if they thought the same thing, though they don't say it. Why is one better than the other?

Think about it. What blacks need if they are going to have the slightest chance in this country is education. We're a high-tech society and getting more so by the week. Either you get the right schooling or you wait tables. Period.

Blacks are badly uneducated. This is obvious as a wart on a prom queen. They don't fumble the SATs because the tests are rigged, but because they don't know the answers. Lockheed doesn't lack black laser physicists because it dislikes blacks, but because there aren't any black laser physicists.

It follows then that if Al Sharpton and Jesse Jackson and the strangely named Kweisi Mfume actually wanted to help, they would be beating the education drum vigorously. Schooling is the only chance blacks have to avoid permanent residence at the bottom of the social heap—or reliance on affirmative action, a shaky prop which fools no one.

Do we in fact hear calls for better schools? Ever see Al Sharpton holding a mass meeting to demand Algebra II? Jesse Jackson thumping the tub for Standard English? How many racial do-gooders of any color, for that matter, have you seen working the ghettos, trying to sell grammar and advanced-placement history? Ever see a March for Calculus? A public meeting trying to get parents to make sure their kids do their homework?

No. Instead, professional blacks tell their people that everything is the white man's fault. Don't turn a gear, they implicitly teach, don't bother to try, because life is rigged against you. Just sit back, feel aggrieved, and passively hold your hand out.

Is this something you say to people you believe to be capable of succeeding? It sounds like David Duke to me.

Now, why do professional blacks play this dismal symphony? Three reasons offer themselves. First, it gets them prominence, an easy living, and probably just a whole lot of women. Second, actually doing anything constructive would be laborious, generate criticism, and take up a lot of Saturday nights. Third, they don't think that blacks can be educated.

That is, the choices are selfishness, cowardice, and racism. Which?

I'm generous. I'll say all three.

Trying to improve schooling for blacks would be a bloody struggle. You would really have to care about the kids to undertake it. The first step would be to get rid of lousy teachers. Many are black. The teachers unions, always protective of their rice bowls, would scream like scalded dogs.

It would take guts to say, "Our kids are more important than your jobs." (Note, by the way, that Catholic schools do a documentably far superior job of schooling urban blacks: Improvement is possible, the professional blacks know it, and still they do nothing.)

You would also have to tell black parents to raise their kids, maybe even to get married. You would have to be willing to expel unruly students who kept everyone else from learning. All hell would break loose at the suggestion.

You would have to do a lot of incorrect things, hard things, even cruel things, that might cut into party invitations. The fancy honoraria might dry up. It looks to me as if the career blacks just don't care enough. In fact, one might conclude that the whole black-leadership thing is a scam.

Am I being unfair? Tell me how.

If it's not selfishness or cowardice, then it has to be racism. By all appearances, the professional blacks figure that their people just aren't smart enough to compete.

The evidence that they believe this is strong, if not conclusive. Notice that the pros demand much from whites, but little from blacks. They want reparations, affirmative action, special privilege, money from lawsuits, removal of the Confederate flag, renaming of bridges, and so on. The underlying premise appears to be that blacks must be protected from competition, not prepared for it.

Now, where is this going to take us? In fifty years, are blacks still going to be at the bottom of every measure of academic achievement? Apparently so. Who will profit from this? Whites? No. Ordinary blacks? No.

But will professional blacks profit?

You bet.

Incidentally, I might ask Jesse and the gang, why am I, a white guy with nothing to gain, sticking my neck out to suggest what you ought to be suggesting? Odd, isn't it? Can I be a black leader?

The Sharptons and Jacksons in fact perpetuate the current racial stasis, which is likely to prove dangerous. Racial relations are not improving. The eerie censorship we call political correctness holds the lid on, yes. Nobody can complain very much, except blacks. The economy is good. All seems quiet. But.

Resentment, hostility one might almost call it, grows among whites. Blacks are already angry. Nobody any longer seems to expect real improvement. Whites mutter about unqualified blacks at work, speculate on the proportion of blacks who can work at a federal agency before it ceases to function.

Meanwhile, it seems to me that despite (or even because of) the symbolic victories of blacks, their political position imperceptibly worsens. Hispanics are about to become more numerous than blacks, and both know it. Hispanics view blacks as competition. They are winning the contest for unskilled jobs.

Further, the economic position of blacks is heavily dependent on affirmative action, which is under attack across the United States. The anger of whites is a carefully overlooked, deliberately unmeasured force of unknown portent. Whites never respond to political attack, haven't yet anyway, but some rubber bands are better not stretched.

If an economic downturn comes along, if Hispanics rise too quickly, if racial preferences go away, if the veneer cracks—I want to be somewhere else.

51

Just Because They Aren't Out To Get You Doesn't Mean They Won't

I keep hearing that the government spies on us, or wants to, or can and just needs an excuse. Its purposes are said to be dreadfully nefarious, usually the establishment of a dictatorship. Our privacy disappears. The Feds probably have a vast listening post in Roswell, New Mexico, where the Air Force stores dead Martians, that spies on us day and night. One soon day, FBI agents in black helicopters will fly through our windows and plant chips in our heads. The gummint is out to get us.

Regarding which, a few thoughts (which come through the chip planted in my head.)

Actually the government isn't out to get us. Technological inevitability is easily mistaken for governmental conspiracy. And that's the problem. You can fight back against a conspiracy. How do you argue against convenience? Or against catching people who run red lights?

For example, the police don't want a national database of photos from driver's licenses, or favor a national ID card, because they want to oppress people. They want these things because they want to catch criminals. The federal agencies of law enforcement and of national security don't want to monitor the Internet for totalitarian purposes. They want to prevent terrorism and impede the traffic in drugs.

At least, that's what most of them want.

Technology that serves these good purposes just happens to be technology that would serve totalitarian purposes.

Herein lies the rub: A conspiracy can be opposed. It is harder to oppose a myriad of databases, each of which is in fact intended for good purposes. It is even harder when the direction of technological advance makes control virtually impossible. The technology of surveillance, or more correctly technology that can be used for surveillance, advances at a breakneck pace. We can't stop it.

And the government will, I promise, use it. Not to enthrone a Hitler, but to constrict gradually, in the name of every imaginable good cause, the times and places in which we will not be watched. This won't be the intention. It will be the effect.

Consider the innocent manner in which privacy diminishes:

Cameras at intersections in my county are now used to photograph automatically the license plates of those who run red lights. There's no conspiracy here. People complained of light-runners. The police didn't have enough officers to watch intersections. Someone suggested using cameras.

Today, only automobiles that run lights are photographed. Today, an officer presumably has to look at the pictures on a screen and write down the numbers. However, it would be just as easy to photograph all licenses. Software exists which, adapted to the purpose, could read the numbers and record them. (Think of common OCR software used in offices.) The justification would be one of legitimate law-enforcement, that the police could enter the tags of stolen cars or wanted criminals. It would indeed serve this purpose.

The same system would also allow the government, should it choose, to keep records of who drove where, day or night, month after month. Computers are easily powerful enough.

Today, only a few intersections have these cameras. They will grow in number. It would be easy to install at stop signs little gadgets, mini-Doppler radars or what have you, to cause a light to flash if you ran the stop sign. Or a camera to photograph your license and email you a warning. Optoelectronic companies, with no ulterior motives at all, are developing cameras the size of postage stamps.

Technology gets used.

The Internet is a grave, but apparently innocuous, threat to privacy. Email in many circumstances can be easily, automatically, and undetectably monitored—by the government, by smart teenagers, by commercial enterprises. Tracking your tastes in Internet pornography is real easy. The papers recently carried stories of a company that sells software for listening to music on your computer. It seems that the software, without notification to the user, emailed to the company information, some of it read from the computer's hard drive, on the user's listening preferences.

Among what are called hackers, the secret installation of software to allow reading of files is old news. You can bet the mortgage that the intelligence agencies are very, very good at this stuff. In principle they target the computers of Saddam Hussein and suchlike. Your computer is just as vulnerable, and you would never know that it had happened.

Who if anyone is being watched by whom for what reasons, I don't know. I know with certainty that it is easily possible.

A crucial point is that the accretion of databases and networks is not going to stop. It's too easy, too useful, too convenient, too justifiable. Visa and Mastercard know the time and place of every purchase you make, including the memorable evening at that no-tell motel. Banks keep endless financial records, and the government uses them to watch for money laundering and tax evasion.

Tracking your cell phone will likely be possible soon. Ambulance crews like the idea because people in auto wrecks often don't know exactly where they are. Everything can be networked, linked, searched. And will be. Without ill intention.

Would a warrant be needed to, say, electronically track your goings and comings in your automobile? Who knows? (And how would you know whether you were being tracked?) One may argue that there is no expectation of privacy in driving on the public streets. True, sort of: Certainly a cop can legally stand on the corner and read your tags as you drive by. But when the rising efficiency of computers allows what was done sporadically in particular places to be done constantly everywhere, a fundamentally new situation arises.

A little more of the same is more of the same. A lot more of the same is something different.

Knowing that everything you've ever done, every thing you do, may be watched will inevitably intimidate. Think how a normal conversation changes when someone picks up an extension phone. We all have skeletons in the back closets of our lives. There's no conspiracy, but there doesn't have to be.

We're moving fast into a world nobody has lived in before, and we need to learn how to do it.

52

Compulsory Credit

Dear Mr. Kennen,

I am writing in response to the Plastoblight brochure which I found stuck in my mailbox the other day as I returned from walking my dog—a miserable cur, I can tell you. He barks at postmen and then runs and hides in the woods, which is probably why I received your brochure. You see, the mailman has learned that my wretched dog never really eats anyone. A shame.

Anyway, I assure you that I would be delighted to carry a prestigious Plastoblight credit card with its unlimited line of credit, mere 18 percent annual interest on unpaid balance, eating privileges at 13,000 restaurants and, as you point out, the option of instantly getting $500 of Plastoblight traveler's checks in southern Chad, should the exigencies of travel demand it. Frankly, I have always feared running out of money in Chad. I have also feared running out of money right here, but that is not why I am declining your kind offer of a card.

It was the application, you see. It put me off my feed. In fact, it terrified me, and gave me a quite serious feeling of inferiority, enough so that I considered throwing myself from the nearest building—but then who would feed my dog? You see, Mr. Kennen. A man who owns a dog cannot casually do himself in, or run off to Tahiti. No, he has heavy responsibility.

As I've said, the application disturbed me. For example, one line said, "Currently Employed By," followed by an ominous white space. Unfortunately I am not Currently Employed By—or, as I prefer to put it, I am Currently Unemployed By Me: that makes it sound more assertive and deliberate, don't you think? In this day and age, when self-actualization is important (whatever that may be), assertiveness counts for a lot. Anyway, I am a writer of sorts, and writers are never Currently Employed By. The lucky ones eat regularly. I did not have the courage to write "unemployed" on a Plastoblight application.

Then, Mr. Kennen, there was the line that said, "Mortgage or Rent (To Whom Paid)(1)." I don't pay either mortgage or rent, as either would consume altogether too much money. I live in an apartment of the family house and it pains me to say so. It is certain evidence that I suffer from one of those parental complexes with Greek names, and Plastoblight certainly shouldn't extend credit to a lunatic. At least, I wouldn't.

There was "Auto Make, Year, Model, Financed By and Address." My wife and I drive a 1967 Dodge convertible, which isn't financed by anybody. It is ours. All of it. Even, probably, a perfectly enormous grasshopper that got crushed in the radiator screen, though I know little of the game laws in Virginia. (Come to think of it, the dog may have eaten it, believing it to be his by right of salvage. Once they quit kicking, he is perfectly fearless about grasshoppers.)

Then the application wanted to know the total of all my debts and monthly payments. (To be honest, your otherwise commendable application seemed a bit forward in asking such things of a stranger.)

I have no debts. You should understand that a poor man is wise not to incur debts. They are a blasted nuisance. My practice is to save money until I have enough to buy whatever it is I want, and be done with it, rather than dunned for it (a little humor). This may seem faintly un-American, but I will take my chances.

Plastoblight's drift was clear in all this. My financial affairs are simply too well handled for me to get credit. The first requisite for credit is imminent bankruptcy and a demonstrated inability to live within one's means. Is it not so? If I had a crushing mortgage, two automobiles for which I couldn't pay, various imposing debts, and a character that would embarrass a lawyer, I could shingle my house with credit cards — that is, I could get them if I clearly had no business with a credit card.

Speaking bluntly, but hoping you won't take it personally, I hesitate to deal with a company which would extend credit to such people. This means I have to give up the 13,000 restaurants, the 18 percent annual interest, and the traveler's checks in Chad. I have a dog to feed, at least until he learns to eat postmen. Chad will have to wait. The longer, the better.

Sincerely,
Fred Reed

53

A Talmudic Jump-Shot

I want to be a star center for the NBA, with ten years back pay. Now.

And a rabbi.

As a generic white-bread male, I once opposed affirmative action, and said vicious and insensitive things about its remarkable resemblance to a spoils system. I have seen the error of my ways, however, and hereby recant. We should keep affirmative action, I now believe, but democratize it. Everyone should enjoy the honors and emoluments of proven incapacity.

The flaw with affirmative action is not that it rewards the ineffectual, but that it rewards only some of the ineffectual. It doesn't discriminate even-handedly. Right now, relative preference is given to the relatively incompetent, and absolute preference to the hopeless—but only if they are of the correct race or sex.

Suppose that, say, Samoan Americans score twenty points on the SATs below white applicants for an Ivy League school. Some slight enthusiasm will arise for accepting them—but not much. Twenty points is too niggling a deficit. Maybe the students took the tests with a hangover, and the inability is only apparent.

But if a black student scores 250 points lower that whites, he will be judged almost supernaturally qualified, and stuffed bodily into Berkeley. A white applicant whose academic prospects were equally bleak would be junked.

No sensible or fair-minded person can object to awarding advancement according to competitive incompetence, but the American way is to reward individual disqualifications, as distinct from group incapacities. White males also are individually incompetent in some fields, sometimes disastrously so. Should they not be given preference for those specific jobs they can't handle?

Professional basketball, for example. An unbiased judge would have to conclude that I am preternaturally unsuited to replace Michael Jordan on the Chicago Bulls. I am too short, too slow, too old, too weak. My jump shot, though a thing of beauty, is too independent-minded to go where I tell it. It is true that I am not actually confined to a wheel chair, but I am otherwise a dream candidate for affirmative action.

I want to play center.

Further, I have the collateral credentials, being a victim: The NBA obviously discriminates against white players, or would if it had any. Alas, poor me. How I have suffered.

Further still, I have been a victim for generations. (I'm not sure what that means, but I don't think it matters.) Blacks invariably point to slavery as justification for preference, the mistreatment of a great-grandfather being undeniable qualification for admission to a doctoral program in laser physics. Ah, but white males can make the similar claims.

I too can demonstrate that some of my ancestors were discriminated against, somewhere else, a long time ago, by people now dead, who had no connection to the NBA. (I think a few were burned at the stake or something on St. Bartholomew's Day in 1572. Good riddance, too. Ever meet a Calvinist?)

But I don't stop at claiming the mantle of Jordan. In accordance with the accepted principle of statistical inference of injustice, I want to be a rabbi. Notice that no white Protestant male has ever been a rabbi. Not to criticize the Jews, but...hey, come on, guys: Four thousand years of history, tens of thousands of rabbis, and not one has been a Presbyterian. I'm expected to believe it's a coincidence?

(Incidentally, there has never been a Jewish pope. Clearly an EEOC case. Can the 14th Amendment be broadened to include Italy? Has it been?)

All right, all right. Honesty compels the recognition that those hostile to competent white males do have a case. Feminists for example point out that white males, being sexually insecure and therefore bedeviled by a compensatory obsession with achievement, have selfishly dominated history for ages.

A close reading of history supports them: Such males have invented algebra, geometry, calculus, refrigeration, transistors, television, philosophy, architecture, computers, chemistry, automobiles, vaccines, airplanes, symphonies, washing machines, and the Simpsons (Bart and Lisa, not O.J.)

This egocentric masculine flowering has to be stopped, argue feminists compellingly, and affirmative action is the way to stop it.

Fine. I'm sorry. I apologize. We pale males did do all those things. It was awful of us. We didn't mean it. All I urge is that, now, white male incompetence be equally enriched with everyone else's. Certainly something can be found which each of us guys is unsuited to do.

Me and the NBA, for example. I'll start at four million a year, plus signing bonus.

In conclusion, while there may be minor disadvantages to the universal promotion of inability through a more fair-minded affirmative action, the loss in technical mastery will be more than balanced by the gain in...in...hmmmm. And if you are wheeled into the operating room one day, and see your neurosurgeon standing there with a puzzled look and an ice-cream scoop, well, just have a remedial tag on your toe. ("Open other end.") Think, while you can, of the social benefit.

54

The Questionable Existence Of "Racial Profiling"

Lately there has been considerable honking and blowing in the press about "racial profiling" by the police. People who make their livings by being in an uproar are. Columnists emit boilerplate indignation. Politicians pose. Legislators threaten to pass laws ending this iniquity. Etc. Regarding which, a few thoughts:

If columnists, and a lot of other people, spent time in police cars (I do: I've written a weekly police column for the *Washington Times* for half a decade), they would discover all manner of interesting things. For example, that "profiling" means recognition of patterns. If you call it profiling, or much better, "racial profiling," you can make it sound evil and discriminatory and establish a category of victims.

Not exactly.

To begin with, the imputation of racial hostility without establishing it is dishonest and, often, nonsensical. For example, in Washington the majority of cops are black, and much of the time we have had a black chief. For another, although again you have to have some first-hand knowledge of the police to know this, black cops behave just like white ones.

Cops, who are on the streets forty hours a week, notice consistencies. For example, youngish women, in fishnet stockings and plastic miniskirts up to their armpits, lounging against lampposts in red-light districts, tend to be prostitutes. So the cops check these women out. They do not check out elderly women in minks, or men with brief cases, for prostitution. The police do not have a vicious prejudice against plastic miniskirts. Nor do they hate young women. They simply know from endless experience what kinds of people are usually engaged in prostitution.

This is profiling.

They also know that scruffy homeless-looking men, walking down back alleys in pricey residential neighborhoods, with VCRs under their arms, are quite likely to have stolen the VCRs. So they check them out.

This too is profiling.

Possibly a woman in a Saran-wrap tank top and a thong bikini just likes Saran wrap. Maybe she's wearing a thong bikini because the weather is warm. Maybe she is on her way to a costume party. Or took a wrong turn on the way to the beach. And perhaps the scruffy guy is an eccentric millionaire like Howard Hughes, taking his VCR for a walk. Maybe some charitable rich guy gave a bum a VCR out of the kindness of his heart.

So, yes, you could say that checking out half-naked women on street corners, or derelicts with expensive items, is discrimination. They might be innocent, yes. And it's certainly profiling.

But it is the soul of police work. Scruffy people who go into expensive department stores, in baggy clothes, and then proceed to look furtively around and brush up against merchandise, are often shoplifters. This recognition is profiling. Perhaps they are innocent— honest paranoids, or have merchandise-brushing personality disorder.

But people who work in security in those stores know what shoplifters look like. And so they watch them.

Security personnel at airports look for certain kinds of people—those who fit the terrorist profile. IRS audits people who meet certain standards. On and on. It isn't that airports carry irrational prejudices against people who twitch and sweat and have ticking shoulder bags (or whatever is on the profile: I don't know). If you wanted to sit home and twitch, or if they knew for a fact that the ticking came from an innocent alarm clock, they would have nothing against you whatever.

But they know from experience that certain things give away terrorists. So they check out those people. Do you want them to stop?

Problems arise when the targeted class belongs to a politically sensitive group, especially if it is a racial group other than white. (Although profiling can affect whites. If the police check out a slinky white woman who keeps approaching men in the bar of a classy hotel, she may turn out to be promiscuous heiress, which it isn't illegal to be. She raises Cain because she has been humiliated. And she probably has been.)

What usually makes the news is profiling of blacks. The fact is that most street-level drug dealers in Washington are black. Blacks are heavily involved in transportation of drugs for sale. Should you doubt this, ask any cop of any color. Dealers look and behave in certain ways, and are certain kinds of people. They are black, scruffy, young, hang in certain places, display certain body language when cops are around. So cops check them out.

The downside of profiling is that, while young black males on I95, wearing scruffy clothes and driving rentals with no baggage, are in fact often drug couriers, often they aren't. Sometimes they are innocent kids of black doctors, wearing scruffy clothes because it is the current teenage way of annoying their elders.

These kids get very sick, very fast, of constantly being stopped and humiliated in front of their girlfriends. I don't blame them. Your choice: Let the drugs through to avoid embarrassing the innocent kid, or embarrass the kid and get the drugs. That is precisely the choice. Let's not pretend otherwise.

It is also true, but verboten to point out, that race and crime are very closely correlated. When I go into the security rooms of the big department stores around the Pentagon (usually to pick up a shoplifter), the photographs of previously collared boosters are almost entirely black. The region isn't.

Now, you can explain this correspondence as you like: You can blame society, blacks, whites, capitalists, racists, the weather. You can say it's my fault, your fault, God's fault. The dog did it. But it's a fact, politically palatable or not. Cops deal in facts, not theories.

They check out those who fit the patterns.

Racial discrimination? Seldom. The same majority-black cops who check out likely black drug dealers would just as quickly check out whites if the whites fit a pattern. They assuredly do check out prosperous-looking whites with Virginia and Maryland tags who park in bad black sections of Washington. Anti-white prejudice? Nope. They know they are there, almost certainly, to buy drugs. Whites from McLean don't have poor black friends in Anacostia.

Profiling.

55

Teacheresses Vs. Boys

I've been consulting with the National Football League. I want to learn how to dropkick a radical feminist. It's harder than it looks. They aren't real aerodynamic, so it's a bear to get a good spiral. Hang time is better with the scrawny ones, but you don't get much velocity.

I'm prepared to practice.

What put a burr in my sock was some hair-ball teacher lady in California who I found on the Web.

She was doing her level best, which was probably pretty good, to make being a schoolboy into a social defect and a treatable condition. This is the default position in schools today. One hears constantly that boys don't do well in school. They don't sit still. They aren't worth a damn.

Maleness is a condition to be cured, and probably a Personality Disorder.

A while back I encountered a teacher wearing a button, "So many men, so little intelligence."

(Clever, Sweet Potato. Maybe you'll be the first female chess grand-master since Newton's wife invented calculus.) Want her teaching your son?

This hostility to boys comes out of feminism, which is the belief that if you can't do squat yourself, keep anybody else from succeeding, and that way you'll look good by comparison.

I'm serious as infected melanoma about the default hostility. The teacheresses do not like boys.

Here's a typical example from the schools of Fairfax County, right outside of the Yankee Capital:

"Various studies indicate that boys are less likely than girls to go to college and have lower educational aspirations. Boys receive lower grades, are more likely than girls to be disengaged from school, and are more likely to view school as a hostile environment...Boys are more likely to be suspended or expelled. Boys are more likely to be held back or to drop out of school. Boys are much more likely than girls to be placed on drugs like Ritalin. Boys are more likely to be disciplined by teachers and administrators."

All true. As it happens, the academic sisterhood *does* forget to tell you a few things about the stupidity of boys. Let me give Sweet Potato something to ponder while she chews her cud.

In 1999, the male average on the math SATs was 531. The female was 495. That's not a trivial difference, sisterhood.

Verbal scores? Males 509, females 502. The boys are ahead in both, despite fidgeting, skipping school, and fighting.

A case, at least partly legitimate, can be made that, because more girls than boys take the tests, (563,000 boys and 657,000 girls in 1999) more dumb girls take it and bring down the female average.

OK. Let's look at the numbers of kids in 1999 making 800s, the highest possible score.

In math: Boys, 4815. Girls, 1611.

Now, Sweet Potato, is one of those numbers larger than the other? Think carefully. Take your time.

Stomp once for yes....

Ah, but girls, we all think we know, are better verbally, so it shouldn't surprise one to find far more girls than boys making Verbal 800s.

Boys with 800 Verbals: 3087. Girls: 2828. And more girls take the test. So many men, so little.....

Do you suspect that the SATs are crooked? Biased against girls? Well, let's look at the Graduate Record Exams. Here is a list of subjects in which men have a higher combined math and verbal score than women: Business, Education, Engineering, Humanities and Arts, Life Science, Physical Science, Social Science, Other Fields.

Here is a list of subjects in which women have the higher combined scores:

Uh...heh....ahhh....

Urg.

Not one field.

Putting it simply enough for the purplest-haired Lesbian, in the higher ranges of intelligence, boys blow girls out of the water. It isn't even close. And everyone who works in the field knows it.

Now, the polite thing would be not to mention these awkwardnesses. Why offend women?

If this increasingly sorry country decided things honestly, on individual merit, and didn't give in to ratbag feminists who want to stick their knives in anything male, including children, I'd keep my mouth diplomatically shut. But the ratbags are there. And they're doing all they can to turn boys into sexless, drugged-up, academically crippled zombies.

Why the dislike of boys? Simple. Feminism isn't about fairness. Sure, once it was, when the questions were equal pay and opportunity and so on. Today, feminism is about (1) revenge and (2) power.

Men, always fools where women are involved, make the mistake of thinking that reason and good will must be in there somewhere. They aren't. Feminists want to win. Period.

Do they really think women can hack it in ground combat? Of course they don't. They're zealots, not fools. They resent hell out of what was a masculine culture that didn't want women around, and in fact regarded them as militarily useless. They hate the military, hate its attitudes, and delight in shoving women down the throats of the generals.

The pattern never fails. When they want to persecute "deadbeat dads," and humiliate them, and bankrupt them, do you think they're really concerned about "the best interest of the children"? Be serious.

Ever hear a feminist criticize unmarried brood mares who drop kids by the dozen and can't raise them?

No. They glorify illegitimacy, which is death to kids, especially in the ghetto, and advocate every measure to promote it—because illegitimacy reduces the role of men. They don't care about kids. The vast majority belong in Holland, holding back water, and figure the only good father is a turkey baster.

They hate men. With whom, in a fair fight, they can't compete. And they know it. Which is why they hate them.

Why do heterosexual teachers buy into hurting boys? Intellectually, teachers fall between education theorists and bright cocker spaniels. (Probably closer to the education theorists. The AKC has been doing wonders with spaniels.) If you think I'm kidding look at the GREs for education majors, whose scores are the lowest of all fields, and remember that these are the smart ones.

Not being terribly bright, they are susceptible to progressive thought, which they understand no better than do progressives. They are not well educated, have little notion what education really is, but dimly resent it. The rambunctiousness of boys is merely a nuisance to them, not a part of the human condition—and do you have any idea of the withering scorn a boy kid of fifteen, with an IQ of 160, directs toward a teacher with an IQ of 95? A bright girl will disguise her scorn. A boy's stands out like a weasel in a punch bowl.

Resentment and revenge. Bye. I've got dropkicking practice.

56

Quacking Toward Kandahar

Recently I attended a costume party of what appeared to be several hundred Republicans from the Reagan Administration, which took place in a pricey forested suburb of Washington. The guests were a mixture of Somewhat Important People and a few Very Important People, by which is meant that had they vanished without trace, nobody would ever have noticed. This is a curious aspect of importance, that it varies inversely with the damage that would follow upon one's loss: when the plumbers strike, chaos results, but if the National Security Council ceased to come to work, nothing would happen.

Anyway, I found myself standing in a glossy kitchen covering several acres. Next to me stood an enormous pink rabbit, who perhaps devised economic policy for the nation, clutching a Heineken and chatting with the Lone Ranger, who doubtless hailed from the State Department—which would explain a lot. In the foreground, silhouetted against a writhing sea of varicolored ears, antennae, tentacles, feathers, and further Heineken bottles, was what appeared to be a male prostitute from the plummier days of the Weimar Republic. (Recent administrations have been able to achieve the overall effect without costumes.) I wrapped myself around my drink for security, like an anchovy around its caper.

A short, cherubic lady came ooching toward me through the crowd. My recollection is that she was dressed as an inflatable boat, but this can't be right. Was it true, she asked eagerly, that I was a Military Writer? Some thought so, I replied, and others didn't. Oh, *wonderful*, how very *perfect*, and did I know the Afghan guerrillas were her hobby? Perhaps this wasn't her word, but it was what she meant; at any rate, the revelation did not bode well for the guerrillas. And had I heard of her scheme to help them? The idea was to fly them freeze-dried backpackers' rations in military aircraft extorted from the Air Force under an obscure provision of the law providing for charitable flights in times of national catastrophe. Why this would have any particular effect on the war was not clear to me.

Having to say something, I said that in my estimation the proper study of Russian-kind was Russia, and that the Soviets could work much good by paddling back across the Oxus and raising goats. Or not raising them. The boat, if such she was, decided that I was a fellow spirit and bared her soul to me. In this unveiling I had no choice: she went at it with the reticence of an exotic dancer who wanted dollars stuffed into her garter. Such terrible things are happening in Afghanistan, she said, as indeed they are. The plight of the Pathans aroused her maternal instincts, she said. Soon she was cooing as if to a hurt puppy: "Oh, those poor, poor people, how I feel for them, poor dears...oh, my little fuzzy ducks."

Her little...what? I thought about it carefully. Yes, that was what she had said. Ducks. Fuzzy ducks.

Now, I have known a good many of these guerrillas, and rather like them. They are among the few people mean enough to stand up to the Russians, being courageous, not too complex, joyfully murderous, and quite capable of skinning a prisoner this week and killing him the next. Whatever one thinks of the war, events in that somber land are not amusing, not a fit subject for dilettantes with too little to do. Perhaps a guerrilla movement is not the best focus for the maternal drives of a woman who badly needs a child or a cat.

An astonishing amount of policy in this city is made by people with the complacent arrogance of the rubber boat, by people willing to prescribe for baffling problems they do not understand in remote regions they cannot find on a map. The truth is that most people in this administration could not distinguish between a helicopter and a hand grenade with fewer than a half-dozen guesses. I am reminded of the cartoon showing an English literary fop saying indignantly to his mother, "One doesn't write *about* anything, Mother, one simply writes."

There is nothing particularly Republican about the woman's colossal fatuity. Hobbyism runs rampant everywhere in Washington. The underlying premise here, as important in its utility in saving labor as was the cotton gin in the old South, is that at the higher levels one does not need to understand anything; indeed, the time spent in learning is better used in self-promotion.

For example, an acquaintance of mine is a catamaran liberal, the sort of Presbyterian minister who has a sailboat, believes that God is a pervasive force for community organization, and yearns to boycott South Africa, wherever it is. The man is positively Newtonian in his predictability, a boiling, narcissistic assault on the doctrine of free will. A sort of jackleg sociology I favor holds that a Methodist is a Baptist with shoes, a Presbyterian a Methodist with a Buick, and an Episcopalian a Presbyterian with a stock portfolio.

Somewhere between shoes and Buick, politics tilts from right toward left. A repressed and angry vanity then discovers that celebrity is after all possible, given the proper venues of demonstration; God is quietly dropped as an embarrassment, and crusades fill the gap. Besides, it's boring out in the suburbs. Here is the origin, and substance, of liberal religious politics.

The minister and his wife know nothing whatever about anything at all, fervently attend rallies for Nicaragua, and have all sorts of indignant bumper stickers, which I suspect they view as reference works. I once showed them some slides I had taken of the Marines in Lebanon before the advent of the unfortunate truck.* "How awful," said the wife. "Lebanon...and what ocean is that on?" One simply writes.

Slipping toward the bar through the surging extraterrestrials, I heard someone say, "Dick Allen. Did you see Dick Allen?...Dick Allen was here, I think he left...Lyn Nofziger. Did you see Nofziger?" I didn't have a clue who Dick Allen was, although the name Nofziger brought to mind a particular sort of beard, presumably attached to Nofziger, that I had once seen on television. It didn't really matter who Allen was, or Nofziger. Every couple of years there is a new Dick Allen, who struts and frets, slings his arrows, and dives back into the law firm. The Dick Allens of the world are the generic debris of campaigns, the bits of wood and old bottles that float in and out on the tides of politics.

To normal people, the terrible importance of knowing Dick Allen is hard to grasp. An administration does not consist of normal people. The people who make up an administration seem to have no existence of their own, no particular qualities other than a consuming desire to be obviously important. The danger is that such derivative people, measuring themselves as they do by their propinquity to the radiant candle of the presidency, consumed by a desire not to *do* anything but merely to have influence or its appearance, will not make reasonable decisions. And, of course, the closer to the president they are, the better. Thus the prevalent photographs of Me in the Oval Office, shaking hands with the latest haberdasher to rule the country. Never mind that most presidents, on their merits, would seldom be invited to more than a Shriners' barbecue.

I talked for a moment to a pleasant fellow, a giant clam, who on President Reagan's long march from Sacramento had been a technician of some sort—an advance man, a pollster, someone in the mechanical trades. (People do not make good clams, even when they are from California. At bottom, clams do not have legs.) He was young and vivacious, pleased with his lot, and bright without having a thought in his head. I tried to talk about Nicaragua but found he knew nothing of the Third World, tried to talk of Star Wars** but found that he thought it extremely important without knowing what it was, tried…without success.

"I'm just a politician, I guess," he finally said, clearly proud of being just a politician. He seemed quite aware of having the world by the handles, of having inexplicably but wonderfully reached the top of the heap, and he was having a lot of fun. After spending a few years as minor lawyers and politicians, such as he sweep into office on some presidential bow wave. And they make the great discovery that the exercise of power requires no qualifications. All you need is the power.

Years ago I thought of such people as being Ostrogoths, fingering with brash incomprehension the scrolls of Rome. Now I think it fairer to regard them as children who have taken over the controls of the amusement park.

It is not true that Democrats cannot be distinguished from Republicans. Republicans these days seem brighter than Democrats, and crazier, or at least crazy in ways promising a higher yield.

"Don't you think the MX is crucial?" I heard someone say at the bar.

"Why?" came the sumptuary response. "We haven't even used the missiles we've got yet."

The remark was original with John Lofton, I think, but in any event epitomized a certain outlaw brashness of the current occupiers of Washington. No Democrat would have ventured such a luminously fey thought. The reason is probably that the Democrats must genuflect to so many solemnities as to make mental movement difficult, and a decent insanity virtually impossible. They must reverence the poor and the black while going to great lengths to avoid them; curtsy to the old, the brown, and the female; pretend insouciance with regard to money while accumulating as much of it as possible; eschew elitism while furiously practicing it; and condemn any foreign policy more virile than the international distribution of powdered milk—although, come to think of it, they are against powdered milk.*** Theirs is a hard row to hoe.

Further, I decided, a Republican always looks expensively dressed, even when disguised as an octopus. Democrats look like dope dealers.

Having made a last foray to the hors d'oeuvres tray (it is possible in Washington to live entirely on hors d'oeuvres), I left. Enough is enough, and sometimes too much. If government is not possible, I reflected, neither perhaps is it necessary. And if the citizenry knew how they were governed, and by whom, those with a sense of humor would buy radiation suits and a ticket to Switzerland and the rest would head straight for the Mexican border.

A high school student in sports jacket and bow tie got my car, looking as I suppose Christopher Buckley must. It was true, we had not yet used all the missiles we had, and there was much of worth to ponder in the ornithological interpretation of the Afghan war: All those little fuzzy ducks, grim of mien and bent under machine guns, quacking toward Kandahar.

*The truck bomb used by terrorists to kill 241 Marines in Beirut
**Star Wars: A technologically improbable anti-ballistic-missile system proposed by Reagan and more discussed than built.
***The sale of powdered milk was much condemned because mothers in the third world watered it excessively to make it last and thus starved their offspring.

This piece was originally published in Harper's magazine. Reprinted with permission.

57

Courting The Wino Vote

I figure we should only let intelligent people vote. Yeah. Give people an IQ test when they register. I'll tell you why. The Democrats keep trying to spread the franchise ever more thickly across the country, like peanut butter. They know they have a lock on the witless vote. Everybody should vote, they figure, especially people who don't have a possum's brains.

Winos should vote, and derelicts, and people who live under bridges, and folks too lazy to register, and idiots, and hobos, and schizophrenics who talk to lampposts. It's just so, well, heartwarming and all. It's like, you know, together-heid.

That's why they tried Motor Voter bills, that automatically register anyone who gets a driver's license, and now there's talk about registering people when they sign up for food stamps, and letting them vote by Internet, and of course years back we got the vote for eighteen-year-olds. (Oh good: Policy made by self-absorbed pubescent hormone wads. Why didn't I think of that?)

We haven't seen the end of it, I tell you. As soon as the Democrats think of it, we'll have automatic registration at needle-exchange centers, morgues, and insane asylums. People with Multiple Personality

Disorder will doubtless get lots of votes. I can see the bumper sticker now: "One Little Voice, One Vote." (You think I'm kidding, don't you? Wait.) Granted, there will be complexities. If a guy thinks he's Napoleon, can he vote? He's a Frenchman.

Anyway, the line goes, every year the proportion of people who vote goes down. We have to Save America. We need to encourage Participation.

I have a better idea. Let's don't. There's such a thing as too much democracy.

Think about it. The moral and intellectual dregs haven't a clue what they're voting for, except the party that will give them more of my money. (Let's see, which one would that be?) What earthly good can come from getting people to vote who are too dim to think and too tor-- pid to bother? Explain it to me. Instead of encouraging the unworthy, I figure we ought to discourage them.

Here are my modest suggestions for improving the acuity of the elec- torate. I'm prepared to accept homage from a grateful nation.

First, nobody with an IQ under 110 will be permitted to vote.

Second, literacy tests will be brought back.

Third, no on under the age of 25 will be permitted to vote.

Am I not the throbbing heart of progressivism? When the staff at National Public Radio hear about it, those nice people with the ter- rycloth minds, I bet they'll give me my own talk show.

Bear in mind that half the population is of below-average intelli- gence. (That's the nature of a distribution symmetric about the mean.) The white mean is 100. This is enough to be a Good Person, have a job that contributes something to the country, and find your way home at night. It is not remotely anything to be ashamed of. But neither is it optimum for understanding the importance of basic research in main- taining our lead in technology, or forecasting the ominous trajectory of Pan-Albanian irredentism.

Now you might say, "But Fred, the voters don't make these decisions anyway. They elect representatives to do these things." True. But when voters are not particularly bright, candidates can herd them like sheep. The tactic in elections today is to cower from substance, avoid any sign of intelligence, and treat the public as an Oprah audience. (If I ever hear again, "Mah fella Merkuns, Ah feel yore pine," I'm going to shriek.) A savvy candidate would rather be caught molesting goats than reading mathematics, because the unwashed resent brains.

But with the threshold at 110, candidates might actually have to address the issues. Respect for intelligence might rear its frightening head. The handout lobbies would cease dominating politics. An astute electorate would not bamboozle so easily. In most elections, an astute electorate would form a lynch mob.

As for a literacy test, people who cannot grasp reasonably complex ideas expressed in Standard English may be presumed not to know squat. Ignorance of the issues is not an obvious qualification for voting on them. Besides, given that everyone has an opportunity to learn to read, those who don't bother may be regarded as socially useless, preternaturally lazy, and certain to vote themselves other people's money.

I don't think the depth of the public witlessness is widely understood. People who are not pig-ignorant often do not grasp just how dark are the minds of those who are.

Very dark. Countless polls over the years have shown that 78% of the public doesn't know what NATO is, 67% don't know who fought in WWII, four of five can't name the three branches of the federal government or get the dates of the Civil War within half a century. Go into the urban slums and you will find that huge majorities say that they haven't read a book in ten years. Many never have. See why we get the presidents we get?

In re literacy tests, I'm talking about a straightforward test of vocabulary and reading comprehension, nothing tricky or specialized. You know the kind: "Paramour most nearly means (1) what you cut grass with in Baltimore, (2) a North African who skydives, (3) a love affair between pears, (4) what you need to open in five-card stud or (5) an illicit lover."

Setting the voting age at twenty-five might allow American politics to transcend the maturity of a panty raid. Kids of eighteen have the political acumen of winos, but are awake more, and therefore more dangerous. They might remember to vote. Inevitably they will vote for whatever will most annoy their parents. The adolescent mixture of romantic absolutism, perfect self-confidence and comprehensive mis-understanding of practically everything bodes not well. Let'em grow up first.

Them's my thoughts. Just to be on the safe side, we'll put up signs outside the voting booths saying, "Free Fortified Wine, Eighty Blocks That Way," with a big arrow. Other signs might say, "Really Good Dope, One Mile." Or maybe, "Unwatched Televisions." In some precincts, nobody would vote at all.

58

Loons in Subarus:
The Press Revealed

Lebanon—Bouncing across southern Lebanon is a convoy of 125 reporters, photographers, and TV crazies in 25 rented Subarus, the assembled war correspondents of the western world. Somehow I don't think this is how Ernie Pyle did it. We look like a traffic jam in Tokyo. Photographers dangle acrobatically from windows. Three TV cameras protrude like poorly thought-out plumbing from the car ahead, intently filming a wrecked jeep. A Brazilian TV crew has crawled onto the roof of its car. Arabs stare, deeply puzzled. They have seen any number of armies roaring about, but nothing so quintessentially mad as this.

For six days I have been living in hotels on Israeli borders with this horde. It is like living in a cageful of histrionic tarantulas. Nowhere but in a war zone have I seen such bellicose, courageous, rude, egotistical, preposterously masculine, faintly reptilian rogues, all working hard at being Marlboro Men. A fellow with a codpiece concession could coin money. Heaven knows what the Arabs would think of *that*.

We pull into Nabatieh, a village. The Israeli escorts eye the anarchic bull-headed mob like snappish sheep dogs. They know that everybody here wants to escape and get his Subaru blown out from under him at the front. A war correspondent feels slighted by fate if he is not almost blown up every day or two. To a large degree, they believe they are the actors in this scene, the armies being props. They look forward to sitting in dark foreign bars in the manner of Hemingway at his most excessive and saying, "Yes, bit of a tiff in '82, got my bloody Subaru shot out from under me, ought to bullet-proof the things....happens, you know."

Some Palestinian prisoners are on display for us in a courtyard, so that we can see how beneficently the Israelis treat their captives. The journalists alight in a pack and race toward the alarmed prisoners. The TV guys jog along in pairs, one carrying the camera and the other with a suitcase full of batteries or whatever. Waving their microphones like the tendrils of some underwater beast, balancing cameras on high to see over those in front, they shout incomprehensible questions at the bewildered Palestinians.

The numerical superiority of the press and its lamentable assertiveness combine, as usual, to dominate the scene. One hundred twenty-five irritated reporters—"Hey, hey, outa the way, buddy, I got pictures to take. Hey you..."—engulf and then digest a dozen Christian militiamen on a pair of armored personnel carriers. Nabatieh is now a Press Event. The public will never see this absurd performance, however. Every photographer will carefully frame out the other newsmen, giving the salable impression that he alone was out there in no-man's land.

Bored, I stand with some other reporters next to an Israeli jeep. A framed picture of Yasser Arafat is tied to the bumper. I grin, knowing a GI gag when I see one, but a camera crew begins jogging toward us with its suitcase. The TV types have detected A Visual in ol' Yasser. The Israeli frantically snatches the picture away: If that goes on the satellite to 500 million viewers, right above the license plate of his jeep, he will have a central position before a firing squad.

The reporters are grousing about the TV clowns and how they don't know what news is and how they're always in the way. This is true. Of the major ethnic groups of the news racket, TV types are the most truly pestilential—comparatively. They carry more electronics than the space shuttle, all wired together with their microphones. They need absolute quiet, nobody else in the picture, a lot of time to set up and a long time to shoot. Reporters usually think TV people should be chained in their hotels during a war, and also between wars. This is wisdom.

Finally the Subaru Bureau remounts and heads home. For any other class of people, driving out of a small town would be done in comity and safety. But no. Everybody jumps in his car as if beginning a Grand Prix, backs fiercely into the crowd and spins the tires viciously trying to be first in the convoy. The idea is to be first to the telephones on reaching the hotel. For this they are perfectly willing to run down seven or eight colleagues and a few slow Arabs, and bash into an armored personnel carrier.

Again we bump across southern Lebanon, cameras protruding, Arabs puzzling, a Japanese used-car lot on the move.

This piece was originally published in the Washington Times.

59

The University As Sandbox

I can't stand it. I'm going to Papua-New Guinea to live in a rain forest, and wear a loincloth, and eat big nasty-looking grubs out of rotting trees, and worship airplanes. That way I'll never have to hear about Colorado College and its Legos again.

So help me, the place is using Legos instead of intellectual tests to admit minorities who lack discernible academic qualifications. I'm not making this up. I'm really not. Listen. This is Dave Curtin, the Higher Education Writer of the *Denver Post*:

"Feb. 1—Colorado College, in an effort to attract minority and disadvantaged students, is dumping those stodgy old college-admission exams in favor of a novel Lego-building test for a handful of applicants...The tests are seen as a way to help colleges maintain racial diversity even if racial preferences are eventually banned."

See? I told you.

The school wants diversity. In University talk, diversity means people who can barely read. Why a college might want people who can't read is a mystery, but Colorado College wants them. The entrance test requires applicants to make a robot out of Legos.

Ye gods and little catfish.

The story explains that the tester shows the students, if that's the word I want, a robot made of Legos. The students then take other Legos and see whether they can replicate the robot. The test, Curtin says (give the guy a break: he's just reporting this twaddle) is supposed to measure all sorts of heartwarming qualities, such as initiative and leadership— "qualities that hours-long ACT and SAT tests never quite get at."

I'm going to scream.

Now, sending *qualified and prepared* members of minorities to university is a splendid idea. I'd be willing to pay for it through taxes, to save on welfare and prisons expenses later. Methinks, however, that if you want diversity, the best approach would be to provide good schools, particularly in neighborhoods that are homogeneously diverse, see whether children could be persuaded to take advantage of them, and send the qualified to college. Another idea would be to send diverse students to remedial high school and then send the prepared ones to college.

The worst idea is to pervert what was once a fairly good system of higher education by having the admittedly unqualified play with toys.

How about a little candor? The reason for the Lego test is not what it measures, but what it doesn't: Intelligence, literacy, capacity to analyze, academic achievement, and any faint hope of success in college. It's a dodge.

Now, if I were a victim of this procedure, I would regard the Lego test as abjectly humiliating. Wouldn't you? All the non-diverse applicants (I think of them as "the homogeneity") would be tested on vocabulary, reasoning, mathematics, literature, history, French, and chemistry. The diverse student would get a robot and little plastic blocks with bumps on them.

How condescending can you get? It's positively degrading. If a kid isn't ready for school, sending him to do make-up work is not an indignity. When he finished, he might have a chance. But no: Legos.

Why is it that so much of social policy ostensibly aimed at elevating minorities serves chiefly to divest them of their dignity?

Does this hoopla really help anyone? Students accepted because they are not qualified will of course perform miserably, and so will need a Department of Diversity Studies, whose function will be to give them high grades without requiring anything of them. Upon graduation, they will work for the federal government or, having straight As in Diversity Studies, will sue if they aren't hired as vice presidents of firms they can't spell. The firms will then put them in Minority Relations and write their salaries off as overhead.

Does this make sense?

The prospects for the future are fascinating. Should Colorado College start a department in laser physics, we may expect that diverse applicants will be expected to gain admission by manifesting virtuosity with a yo-yo. Admittedly, the usual entrance examinations overlook this ability. The Department of Chemistry will perhaps require adeptness with Tinker Toys. The Lit Department might want to be assured that the applicant could chew bubble gum.

Is there no end to the solemn fatuity to which schools will descend to admit people who transparently have no business in college? (No. The question is rhetorical.) If the intent is to give degrees to people who can't earn them, why not issue the degree at birth? Or perhaps have a constitutional amendment declaring all citizens afflicted with diversity to be honors graduates from MIT?

The notion of engendering competence by fiat is not new. Years back, a local jurisdiction decided that it would compulsorily mix the brightest kids in secondary school in classes with the dullest. Heartwarming: No doubt about it. It was also a damn fool idea. These qualities are the two requisites for any policy in education.

I imagined the resulting classes in, say, math. Teacher: "Sally, the first derivative with respect to x of the product of functions u(x) and v(x) is u(dv/dx) + v(du/dx). Bobby, if Mommy Beaver has three sticks, and Itty Bitty Baby Beaver has two sticks…"

The amusing thing is that everyone knows that examination-by-toy is ridiculous. Is anyone in the United States not snickering? The *Denver Post* describes Colorado College as prestigious, which it may have been until February 1. Do you believe that the normal students will regard the Lego kids with respect? Do you think the admittees-by-Lego won't know it?

I have a suggestion. I will donate it to the country without royalties. Let's concede that no more than perhaps a quarter of our young have the intelligence and academic curiosity to go to college. Let us also admit that a watered travesty of a university degree is in fact of little relevance to most jobs. Therefore it shall henceforth be mandated that only those jobs whose actual substance demands education beyond high school shall require a degree.

Then we can stop sending the unable and uninterested to universities that have to be gutted to allow the entrants to appear to be doing what they aren't.

And now I'm out of here. I have to pack my loincloth and chow down on those grubs. They're like bug sushi. A 747 comes over at sunset, and we're having twilight services.

60

Rape Fantasies And Mutant Frumps

I'm gonna smack'em, I tell you. Radical feminists, I mean. I'm gonna take a ball bat to'em.

No. Wait. Better idea. I mean, this country *invented* the wood-chipper. And there's always a market for cat food.

What astonishes me is how feminists have managed to poison relations between men and women. Somehow they have created a nightmare world that doesn't exist, an atmosphere of weird paranoid hostility, and made women, or a lot of women anyway, believe they live in it.

The other day I saw some mutant frump on television. I think it was Patricia Ireland, but it could have been Shamu gone bad. Anyway, she looked like a fireplug with leprosy, and she was hollering about how men were always battering women. (Stray thought: Ever notice that these gals are either butt-ugly or gay as Easter bonnets, or both?)

Feminists are always hollering about how women are battered, beaten, raped, underpaid, bruised, scorned—how women crawl in gutters, pleading for help, struggling piteously, while men—*men*—stand over them in hobnailed boots, grinning and saying, "Har har har."

Don't the men you know do that?

These fantasies rely on battered-women studies, usually written by academic feminists. (Incidentally, friends whom I trust implicitly tell me that Ph.D. doesn't really stand for Purple-Haired Dike. I don't know why not.) They typically say that four out of five women are battered three times every five nanoseconds. Or seven of eight, or nine of ten. It doesn't matter.

Actually, I can hardly get any work done, being so busy battering my daughters and girlfriends. It's a burden. I hardly have time to molest my children. (Six out of every four men molest their children.)

It's nonsense, as a cursory examination of the evidence easily shows. But who examines evidence?

Then there are the feminist rape fantasies, much in vogue with co-eds seeking an outlet for hysterical romanticism. The average feminist couldn't get raped on a troopship with a gallon of bourbon, but never mind.

I recently read a study claiming that one in two women will be a victim of rape. Sure. And I'm Lady Jane Grey. Think about it. Does this mean that one in two men is a rapist? Or are there a few really *busy* guys out there? None of this stuff is true, which doesn't matter at all.

Do women believe it? The other night I was in a bar with a buddy who has wearied of this stuff. He turned to three pretty women playing pool and asked, "Hey, have you been raped?" They looked surprised. Maybe it's not a standard pick-up line. He explained about the studies. They didn't see much sense in it. "That's nuts," said one correctly. Another's comment was a sardonic "Raped?... Not that I remember."

Oh, lord—I can see the headline: "Study reveals that nine of ten women don't remember being raped."

The truth, plain as zits on a prom queen, is that feminists are a hate group, like the KKK or the Baader-Meinhof Gang, only probably loonier. (Feminutsies.) (Sorry. It's late.) They are liars, and verge on crazy. And they're chronically furious.

They don't want to be women, and can't be men, and so compromise on being disagreeable.

Above all else they hate the thought of women having sex with men. At the University of Michigan, maybe it is, there's a bilious woman named Catharine MacKinnon. Kitty Mac is a nice-looking babe when she keeps her mouth shut, which isn't often, and has a certain patrician charm that I associate with jock itch. I find by her this, appalling for its sheer prissiness:

"Compare victims' reports of rape with women's reports of sex. They look a lot alike…In this light, the major distinction between intercourse (normal) and rape (abnormal) is that the normal happens so often that one cannot get anyone to see anything wrong with it."

I guess Kitty Mac and I date different classes of women.

To a feminist, everything sounds like rape. Peanut butter sounds like rape. Wallpaper sounds like rape. The dew on the flowers of morn sounds like rape. I note in passing that Kitty Mac speaks of sex with men as an alien concept, as if she knew of it by dispatches from a distant front.

I think feminists hate the idea of normal sex because they regard men as poachers.

The feminists have persuaded us that even an office is a dark and dangerous place. Yep. Here we encounter Sexual Harassment, which amounts to absurdity as a rationale for Stalinism. Don't you love it? Rape lurks by the water cooler. Bob the comptroller, with the love-handles and wry sense of humor, harbors the lusts of Jack the Ripper. Jimbo tells blonde jokes. Clearly he hates women. He probably melts Barbie Dolls for a hobby. Peril is everywhere. We must be vigilant or the boogeyman will leap from the supply closet.

Unfortunately this stuff has gotten serious. If a man tells a dirty joke, or if a woman who doesn't like him says he did, he can lose his job. We have sensitivity training so that men won't say anything damagingly impure. It's because women don't know about sex. Nor do they have dirty thoughts.

A woman I know said recently that when she entered a room full of guys at work, laughing and talking, they fell silent. She was puzzled and hurt. I wasn't puzzled. So many women have chips on their shoulders, and the penalties for offending them are so great, that silence is the wise course. Is this what we want?

You might be surprised at how many men—including to my knowledge, admirals, generals, the editor of a major newspaper—won't let women into their offices without having a witness present. Bureaucrats in Washington live in an atmosphere of (I apologize in advance) fear and loafing, afraid to discipline female subordinates who don't do their jobs. My buddy the scuba-instructor won't help female students put on their gear. I doubt that one woman in 50, or one in a hundred, would charge that he groped her, but all it takes is one neurotic.

Trouble is, nobody has the moxie to tell these scrofulous tarantulas to bugger off. Which is well for feminists: If people started laughing at them, the whole shebang would collapse in ten minutes.

And they probably wouldn't even make good cat food.

61

The Great Fizzled Playboy Undersea Photo Shoot

It was three a.m. in late December and I and Stu Miller, a federal lobbyist and former motorcycle racer, were zooming around the DC beltway in his male-menopause red Miata and discussing what to do for the Millenium. The possibilities were dismal.

"God, some black-tie thing on the Hill? I'd rather slit my wrists," Stu said.

"I'd much rather slit your wrists. Let's blow it off and go diving."

We're scuba loons. Blowing it off and doing something else is my response to most of Washington.

"Yeah," he said, attempting humor, "We can dive in black tie…Hey…*Hey!*"

The idea burst on us like a squeezed grape. "What if we really dive in black tie? Take a bottle of champagne. Take photos…."

The light was dawning hard. Stu nearly hit a tree.

"…We'll take the millenium *Playboy* down with us, sell them the shots. Yeah."

"The magazine will get soggy"

"Not if we laminate it. I'm gonna call *Playboy*."

Right, I thought. Sure. The idea was admittedly cute, and we'd both written for *Playboy*, which might add to our credibility, especially since the editors didn't know us. On the other hand, magazines work months in advance. We'd have to leave town in four days for the Keys. At bottom we didn't have a corn dog's chance in a hog trough.

Sure enough, *Playboy* responded that it was thinking about the idea, which is magazine-talk for we aren't thinking about it but don't want to crush your spirit. By then we were committed. We were going to do it anyway. We packed several cubic yards of scuba gear into a station wagon and pointed it down I-95 toward Miami.

All the way down we fantasized. What if we did the shoot and just sent the pics to *Playboy*? God worked in strange ways, we said. And with strange people, which gave us a shot. What if…what if…?

You gotta understand. When we were growing up, or at least in college getting older, *Playboy* was our philosophical guidebook. We all thought we ought to be at the University of Virginia, look like a young William Buckley, and drive a Lamborghini. *Playboy* gave us the polish, if not the Lamborghini. It was where we learned who Mancini was, what existentialism meant, and how to behave around people who wore shoes. We dreamed of Vargas girls and wanted to be like Hugh Hefner, to whom we referred familiarly as Hef. *Playboy* actually sophisticated us. And we really did read the articles. Too.

So the thought of actually being in the magazine—having a photo of us in black tie with champagne and lovely babes in the altogether or at least mostly together—wow! Sure, a wetsuit had the erotic appeal of a cold shower. Maybe a reef wasn't a blues club in Chicago. But we were talking image. And as a glittering male ego-fantasy, it was up there with Marlboro Man, or a restored '57 Chevy with 454 cubes and a mild blower and 73 coats of hand-rubbed Kandy-Kolor cherry metal-flake lacquer.

Even though it wasn't going to happen.

We made 800 miles the first day, 300 the second, and pulled into Key Largo in early afternoon. Hotels were insanely pricey because of the Millenium. We went back up the road to Florida City and got a room in the Econo-Lodge near the Last Chance Saloon, a biker bar in which we felt at home.

For the next two days we dived in the mornings to check our gear and figure out how to do a shoot under water. I'd used a camera in the ocean enough to know that I couldn't. We needed a cheap photographer. We found one.

In the afternoons we got props. OfficeMax laminated the cover of the Millennial *Playboy* for us. Fortunately it was brightly colored for good contrast against a midnight ocean. The centerfold was trickier. We did it in two parts and taped them together.

Then we got plastic "Happy New Year 2000" party hats and cheap red cummerbunds and bow ties (something told me the resale value would be marginal), a bottle of incredibly lousy champagne called *Dom Bahde Stufe* or something, with a gaudy label, and a box of frozen peas to attract fish for local color. (Hef probably didn't do this at his parties. Well, we were going to.)

Since *Playboy* wasn't going to happen, we laminated the cover of *Soldier of Fortune* magazine, for which I once worked in another and stranger life. The editor, Bob Brown, was a buddy of mine, and I knew he'd run it. We wanted a published record.

OK, Plantation Key, nine-thirty on New Year's Eve. We showed up at Conch Republic, a dive operation running a reef trip for people who wanted to be underwater at midnight. The photographer showed. Seas were flat, the night warm. We loaded gear, boarded, and went to Davis Ledge, a nice easy reef at thirty-five feet. The other divers suited up and went in. Stu and I looked like idiots in cummerbund and party hats. We probably were idiots, so it didn't bother us. He went in. I followed.

At which point everything went wrong.

His hat tore in two in mild chop. The centerfold slipped from our hands. He dropped the *Dom Bahde Stufe*, having forgotten that he'd need one hand free to clear his ears. We finned around the bottom like neoprene bats and found it. The photographer had vanished. We followed the reef and reacquired him. He looked unhappy.

His camera had flooded.

It was definitively the end of our great all-time wet dream of glory, of our quest for ultimate meaning, the closest we would ever come to the Playboy Mansion. True, the magazine wasn't interested—but what a photo for the office wall.

What the hell. The water was clear and lovely, the reef burning in reds and orange where our lights touched it, goofy fish slowly swimming and wondering what we thought we were doing. We stayed down for forty-five minutes, surfaced, had (good) champagne and shrimp on the boat, and started back.

Ashore, I went to the car and found a message on my cell phone. My daughter, I figured. She was at the Phish concert in the everglades.

It never occurred to me that it might be *Playboy* calling.

And it wasn't. It was my daughter.

But…it could have been *Playboy.* We wuz almost contenders, but heartbreak got there first.

The Last Chance saloon was rocking. Bikers and local watermen were partying with their ladies, and a country jukebox was wailing laments about sorry paychecks and bad divorces. Stu and I were on our fourth Rum Runner, a devastating drink for whose acquaintance we would pay dearly in the morning. It didn't matter. Nothing mattered.

"Y'all want two more?" asked the barmaid.

"Yesh. Rum Runners. Hold the Runner."

We stared at each other in sorrow, trying not to put our heads on the bar and sob. It isn't a good thing to do in biker bars.

62

Bogart, Gore, and Desperation

Whooh! I've been working like three donkeys on Texas crank, trying to decide which empty jar I want for President: Al Gore, or George W. Gore. Mostly I come up dry. It's not easy even to know which is which.

I'm starting to narrow the choice, though. It's either Humphrey Bogart or Carl Perkins, on a write-in. I guess I'll go with Perkins. I've been a low-down, Southern, hotrod teenager, dating girls whose daddies had shotguns behind the door, and that's what ol' rockabilly Carl sings about.

Except he's dead.

Anyway, we gotta do something about this president mess. I'm real tired of New Age presidents who look like bulk-pack bean curd that a mad scientist spilled something radioactive on, and it crawled out of the package and started shaking hands. Eight years of the National Embarrassment from Arkansas have strained my tolerance. I don't want another pasty guy with the character of a damp Kleenex, except you can't wipe up spills with him.

Which has led me to a brilliant idea. Since we don't have Presidents any more—they're more like human place-holders—why not have a virtual President? Do him in software. We could have anyone we wanted.

Like Perkins. One good thing about those Fifties rockabilly guys was that there wasn't a whole lot ambiguous about them. You knew who they were. They wore maybe leather jackets and biker boots and they had hair. It was before the days when delicate guys wore Brylceem and looked harmless. (Remember? "*A Little Dab'll Do You.*" I guess a man's dot of goo is a man's dot of goo.)

If you tell anybody I sank to that, I'll bomb your house.

Anyway, a good country singer wore about eight pounds of AceHold Dura-Grip pomade that set like concrete, and dated women who looked like Dolly Parton. None of them would have married a walk-in refrigerator the way Willy Bill Clinton did. They were people you could heist a brew with, and not want to wash your hands afterwards.

That's really what I'm getting at. We need a better class of reprobate to mismanage the country. I've been around the Yankee Capital a day or two now, and met a passel of politicians, and have yet to meet one I didn't instinctively want to kick hell out of. You see them at receptions on the Hill. They glance kinda sneaky at your name tag so you won't see them doing it, and then they say, "Fred! So good to see you." You could wear a tag that said, "This End Up," and they'd say, "*This!* So good..." Then while they talk to you they look over your shoulder for a more important name tag. It's a Thousand Yard Stare. I used to think they had something wrong with their eyes.

Bogart wasn't like that. You knew he was going to do what was right and anybody who didn't like it could chew on a forty-five caliber slug. By contrast, you can just tell that Al Gore would drown his mother in Valvoline to get elected. Besides, he looks like two yards of fatback stuffed into a suit.

Bogey had a certain compulsive honesty about him, even when he was playing crooks. You can't imagine the guy working the rubes at a PTA meeting: "Yes, ma'am, I am de*vot*ed with mah entire *be*-ing to whatever dumb-ass idea you just said. I *assure* you that I *live* for nothing else." (They talk in rhythm. It dulls the listener's mind.)

People had more backbone in Tennessee roadhouses in 1952. I know because sometimes I watch really terrible movies after midnight. In those movies Jake Gumbo, the local bad boy who really had a heart of gold, would pull up to Mike's Sublime Inn out on some winding road in his 48 flathead Ford with big dice on the mirror and a cigarette hanging out of his mouth and a mound of pomade on his head with some hair in it.

You knew the bad guys by the pool table were going to start mistreating the female lead. She was sitting at a back table, all helpless innocence like you usually find in women in Tennessee roadhouses. The toughs would give Jake the hard eye. He'd give it back and light another cigarette. The bad guys would start to abuse the gal. Jake would pick up a pool cue with a kind of focused look. He knew what was right.

Can you imagine Al Gore doing that? He wouldn't even try to save Lauren. He'd probably steal her lingerie.

Our whole government is just plain embarrassing. Jake Gumbo for President, I say.

There's a way out of this trap. We'll do presidents in software.

I saw a show about a computer in Hollywood that was simulating Bogie. They had fed his voice and his face from all angles into a computer, and then they sort of projected him onto an actor. It was like having Bogart alive again. Same expression, same gravelly voice like he'd been chain-smoking Camels with Drano in them. The announcer said that one day actors wouldn't act any more. They'd just rent their personalities. A studio would get Clint Eastwood on a floppy disk.

I figure we could do that with presidential candidates. Only we'd invent them from scratch. You could have software called GooberMaker or something, and each party would get a copy. When it loaded, the screen would show a featureless proto-president with no characteristics, which is what they seem to have done this time anyway. You'd have an on-screen editing page with sliders for Assertiveness, Masculinity,

Caring, Sincerity, and so on. You could plug in the polling numbers hot from a modem.

For women who wanted a non-threatening candidate, the software would make the face chipmonkish and cute. You'd just know he thought a lot about feelings. If times were tough, and a blush of testosterone was thought suitable, five o'clock shadow might subliminally suggest adroitness with a tire iron.

There would be check boxes, see. Eyes: Steely, melting, glazed, crossed. Walk: Confident, Swagger, Strut, Swish. You could store settings for different audiences. If the campaign staff were going to play the software for a society of birdwatchers, maybe the candidate could grow feathers. Who knows? How about pre-set spin control: "I...did...*not* ...have sex with that: (intern, ambassadress, ambassador, Socks.)"

It beats what we've got. So does the average fence post.

63

Patenting Emily

Director, US Patent Office
Washington, DC

Dear Sir:

I want to apply for a patent on a Perpetual Motion Machine. I know the Patent Office declines to accept such applications on the grounds that perpetual motion is physically impossible—but has the Patent Office met my daughter Emily Anne? She is eight months old, and I assure you that she is in perpetual motion. In fact, "perpetual" seems an underestimate, and "motion" is a weak word to describe the phenomenon.

Yesterday, for example, she pulled a bowl of soup into my lap at a restaurant. While I struggled to clean up the mess with her in one arm, she cooed and began hitting me in the face with a handful of salad. She is a charming little thing, Mr. Director, but I didn't really need the olive oil on my glasses. Then she started alpining up my chest, using my shirt pocket as a toe hold. Her ambition is to sit on her daddy's head.

This may seem a small goal, but she is a small girl. So far. I don't suppose she gains more than a pound a day, but it seems like a lot. Do you think I am rambling? You will see immediately how this is related to my patent application. If she is in perpetual motion, and her mass increases, so does her momentum. You may find this interesting. I find it frightening. After all, it is my head that is to be sat on.

Anyway, as I was saying, she could have worse goals. I mean she could dream of reconquering the Sudetenland or of sweeping out of Asia with a million Mongol horsemen at her back and overrunning Russia. Can you imagine how history would have been changed if the Mongols had suffered the misfortune of capturing Emily Anne?

First she would have sat in the middle of the camp like a happy little teapot and complacently charmed the troops into mush. She is not much impressed by Khans, whether Golden or of pot metal.

Then she would have rampaged about, blunting swords, tearing the feathers from arrows, and gnawing horses on the fetlocks, or flintlocks, or whatever those parts are. The effects of perpetual motion on a barbarian army would be terrible, I am sure. You can imagine the horde investing Novgorod and saying by messenger, "Send forth a baby sitter, now, or we'll sack the joint."

She crawls now, like Man of War in the stretch, and she is giving up naps. In short, she is getting both perpetualer and motioner. If she gets faster and keeps it up longer, I may need two patents just to keep track of her. If we turn our back on her for a moment, she is off and sailing down the hall, and heaven only knows where she will turn up. Generally, she is not hard to find. The crash of glass is a distinctive sound.

Should you have any doubts about the perpetualness of her motion, you could have the staff of Lawrence Livermore or Fermilab examine her. The danger, however, is that she would examine them. The average physicist is not accustomed to dealing with forces of such magnitude, and may require hospitalization and a new tie.

The better approach would be to send someone from one of those Floridian sideshows where they specialize in wrestling octopuses underwater. As nearly as I can tell, she has more arms, but this would be the wrestler's problem. Should she ever hold still, I will count them.

As for practical applications, I suggest the Pentagon. There is something Napoleonic about Emily Anne. She looks at the world with an expression of complacent, condescending superiority very like that of the little Corsican in portraits, although she does not stick one hand into the front of her nighty. Instead she grabs the nose of whoever is nearest and peers at it clinically. If Napoleon had done this, he would have been far more feared.

I believe it is proper to enclose engineering drawings with a patent application. Emily Anne is not drawable—have you ever tried to draw at a dead run, while avoiding broken vases and wiping olive oil from your glasses? However, I have some photos of her taken at the beach. The blur in the left foreground—next to the fallen umbrellas and overturned picnic basket — is Emily Anne. It is a good likeness.

Sincerely,
Fred Reed

64

Sour Thoughts on Multiculturalism

I guess somebody needs to explain multiculturalism to me. It's because I'm from West Virginia. We're slow up in the mountains, and dim, and have trouble understanding things that don't make any sense at all.

Be patient. Explain multiculturalism to me in block letters.

If my history's right, all kinds of folk used to come to America from every whichaplace. (I'm not sure that's a word, even in West Virginia.) They'd go off to a ghetto and be miserable. You'd have Eye-talians and Irish and Jews and Scowegians, people from every place there was and probably from some there wasn't. Weren't.

Before long they'd start marrying right and left, apparently without looking. Pretty soon you had people named Heidi Torricelli O'Feinstein. They weren't sure what they were any more, so they decided to be Americans and not worry about it. It made good sense, because America was where they were.

This gamboling about in the gene pool produced accidental mono-culturalism, and it worked pretty well. Hostilities died out because they were too complicated to remember. I mean, if the Germans were supposed to hate the Poles, and you were half German and your grandmother was a quarter Polish, then you had to hate an eighth of your grandmother—and no man could tell which eighth. The accounting alone made it impractical. People began to get along because it was the easy way out.

It works still. I'm mostly English, and months have gone by since I've shot at an Irishman.

But now, if I understand aright, we're going to be multicultural, and stay split up in different tribes and act like it's a good idea. (Separate but equal. Didn't we do that before?) We're going to have white, black, Hispanic, and Asian nations all in the same country. And we're all going to live together in peace and love and mutual respect, and have drumming circles and smoke ditchweed together.

Now, granted I'm simpleminded. I don't understand higher psychology. My school learning is pretty weak, like moonshine that didn't get run through the radiator enough. Still, before we get too multicultural, I figure we ought to see how it works for other folk.

Start with Canada, since it's stuck to us and can't get away. Canada has a pretty good dose of Frenchmen in Quebec, and they've been nothing but trouble. The country's always about to break apart because nobody can stand the French, and the French hate everybody. They'll never get used to each other.

Now, you might think, OK, that's just the Canadians. Maybe their brains froze or something. Maybe multiculturalism works better for other people.

Well, how about Mexico, which is multicultural in Indians? Last I heard, Mexicans and Indians were having a shooting war in Chiapas. So far, they haven't done much in the line of drumming circles. Maybe some scalpings, though.

Of course there's Yugoslavia, the world's motingator case of multiculturalism. You can't get much more multicultural. They've got cultures nobody can spell, all cutting each other's throats. So far they've produced nothing but shrapnel.

I begin to suspect that multiculturalism works fine, soon as one side kills the other off.

And in Indonesia the Indonesians butcher the East Timorese, and in Rwanda the Tutus chop up the Hutsis (or Tootsies, or somebody), and in the Sudan the Moslem northerners kill the southern animists, and Iraq gasses its Kurds. In Malaysia the Malays can't stand the Chinese.

In Ireland the Protestants and Catholics think they have to blow each other up every little while, like leaky air mattresses. The Vietnamese kick around the Montagnards, the Cambodians slaughter their Vietnamese, the Japanese hate their Koreans, and in South Africa the whites and blacks claw at each other like cats in a bag.

In Israel the Arabs and Jews are no end multicultural, between explosions. The Christians and Moslems go at it in Lebanon, and the Guatemalans torture their Indians, the Tamils and Sinhalese in Ceylon shoot each other in droves, and...

Yep, this multiculturalism business works pretty well. No one can deny it. Pretty soon there won't be anybody left.

While we're at it, how has multiculturalism done in the U. S. of A.? So far, it's the worst problem we've got, unless Hillary gets elected. We have a white European country with an utterly incompatible, inassimilable black African culture spread through it. We spend most of our national energy trying to straighten that one out. We've got crime, welfare, racial hatred, riots, burned cities, weird political stuff like affirmative action, constant lawsuits, fear, loathing, and ill will.

I don't guess we better try any more multiculturalism just yet. We don't have enough guns.

But that's just me. I hear now we're gonna ghettoize the Hispanics instead of assimilating them, so we can have more riots and cities going up in flames, and about a dozen generations of hostility, and car bombs if we get really multicultural. Hooboy. I've never heard of a better idea.

Except any other idea at all.

Fact is, people of different flavors just don't get along very well. Maybe we ought to. Maybe we all ought to love each other. Maybe we ought to be reasonable, though that's stretching it. But we aren't going to. We never have. So we better get busy and try to be one kind of people. That would be the smart thing to do. Still, it's worth a try.

Why do we deliberately adopt a guaranteed recipe for divisiveness? You'd think a track record of unrelieved multicultural disaster would be some slight contraindication to more of it. If you think that, you obviously don't have any experience of American politics. Still, you might ask, who is it that wants to inflict a multicultural morass on innocent Americans?

First, Democratic politicians trying to lock in voting blocs.

Second, the whole lemming pack of post-hippie professors, intellectuals, feminists, self-serving racial dissensionists, and aggressive vegetarians who have the touchiest of feely ideas and thirty seconds of experience in the real world. Thirty seconds aggregate, I mean. Why are they doing it?

Hard to say. They give me the impression of never having gotten over adolescence. They've confused America with their parents, and they're mad at it, and they're throwing a fit.

Me, I'm going back to Wheeling, where people are monocultural and talk the same and have the same DNA, and shoot pool in low dives. I mean, a bar fight at least makes *some* sense.

65

Miracles, Elvis, And Crop Circles

I guess we gotta figure this miracle thing out.

Sometimes I watch the magazine shows on the Spanish television channels to resuscitate my Spanish. Usually they have a story about a miracle. Normally Juan Valdez has seen the likeness of the Virgin of Guadeloupe in his tortillas, or in a water stain on a rock, or somewhere a portrait of Jesus is crying real tears. Word gets around. Thousands of people come to look. The press follows.

Now, as best I can tell, a miracle means anything people don't understand and they can't do again to study it. Miracles seem to be all over the place, like ticks on a summer cow. They just flat gum up the grocery-rack tabloids.

Most religions have miracles. Jews have the parting of the Red Sea, and Christians have the turning of water to wine (which seems to me a more practical sort of miracle, but then I don't have Egyptians chasing me), and the Moslems have the ascent of Mohammed to heaven. India's a regular mass market in miracles. Ancient Rome had so many they had to store them in warehouses.

Then you have secular miracles, like Elvis sightings, UFOs that do weird sexual examinations of hysterical spinsters, magical pyramids that sharpen razor blades, mutilated cattle, funny-looking space aliens with bulgy gray heads that the Air Force stores in New Mexico, and crop circles.

Reporters always treat believers, whether in the Bible or UFOs, with wary condescension, viewing them as witless but numerous, and likely to raise hell if sneered at, so maybe we better not, quite.

Well, maybe. I'm not so sure we have this odd world entirely figured out. I don't know chicken fat about miracles. But just for grins, suppose that something miraculous, or at least inexplicable, really happened, in an ordinary setting.

For example, there's a place called the Washington Sailing Marina, where I go to heist a brew with friends and keep an eye on the Potomac. Suppose that a giant green leprechaun, six feet tall, appeared on the dock. (That's a pretty healthy leprechaun, but the diet's been good in Ireland since the Potato Famine. We'll probably see leprechauns in the NBA.) Suppose he walked out on the river, turned into a huge order of barbecued ribs, and disappeared into the sky like a bottle rocket, *bang!*

Remember we're supposing it really happened. What would the response be of the, say, 25 people who might be there?

Fifteen of them wouldn't see it at all. They'd be looking the other way, scratching, or swilling beer and lying about their stock portfolios. Some would watch, startled, and then begin to worry about themselves, and head for a serious bar. They wouldn't say anything, to anybody, ever. I mean, you don't run up to strangers and say, "Hey, did you see a giant green guy turn into a plate of ribs?" They'd call for a struggle buggy and some big orderlies.

A few would see it together.

"Jeez...Fred, what's *that?*"

"Green guy. No, rack of ribs. No, looks like a bottle rocket."

"Fred!"

"I don't want to think about it."

There would be a lunge for explanatory security blankets. It was a mirage caused by odd reflections on the water. Not ribs, but a flock of seagulls browned by the smog. A Navy submarine, towing a green weather balloon from beneath the water (which is eight feet deep).

That would be the end of it. Nobody would ever speak of it again. It wouldn't have happened.

Even though it had.

Suppose by contrast that the senior class of Tuscaweegee High were at the deck on their senior trip, having a Washington Experience, and saw the ribs make their way heavenward. Suppose the girls started shrieking and latched onto the boys for security, and the boys started thinking they ought to get some leprechauns in Tennessee if that's the effect they had on girls. And suppose they carried on so much that someone called the media.

We still wouldn't know about it.

A TV crew would show up from Channel Zero, two camera donkeys and a blonde reporteress, all bored out of their skulls. They'd be the crew who did filler for News Alive At Five—car crashes, grade-school shootings, and heartwarming stories about a dog that got run over, but survived due to a sustaining faith in multiculturalism.

I can imagine the assignment being made at the studio:

"Hey, Rita, get down to the Marina. They got leprechauns."

"What?"

"Yeah. They fly, like bugs. Yeah, you have to. I know you did Naked Lesbian Pudding Wrestling last week. Go anyway."

The crew would show up and the blonde would ask patronizing questions tipped with humor. "Now, what size were these, uh, leprechauns? Do you see them often?"

The high school kids would be embarrassed and not very credible.

When the segment aired the anchor would trot out a psychologist who would intone, "Well, Roger, it has all the symptoms of mass hysteria."

"Mass hysteria" is psychology talk for, "We're clueless, but if we use a ponderous name and don't look too vacuous, maybe nobody will notice."

In short, if it shouldn't have been there, psychologists will assure us that it wasn't. Actually, a bunch of people can't all see the same thing unless (a) they're telepathic, or (b) it's there. But never mind.

And that would be that. Humorous filler. Even though it really happened.

Further, if a thing isn't repeatable, science can't tell that it happened. This means that if miracles did occur, or do occur, or for that matter anything screwy and not real possible that only happens once, and stops, we can't know it. Science can't tell whether Elvis really materialized in a glowing cloud of Ace-Hold strawberry pomade, or a leprechaun turned into ribs.

To figure anything out, scientists would have to put the leprechaun in a lab with a mass spec and a gas-liquid chromatograph and do PET scans and MRIs, and stick purees of him into a DNA sequencer. And that leprechaun would have to be there every time they looked, which isn't how leprechauns are. Sometimes they're there. Sometimes they aren't.

See? We can't know about leprechauns, if any. As someone said, there are more things in heaven and earth than are dreamed of in our televised drivel. Or, as JBS Haldane put it, the world is not only queerer than we think, but queerer than we can think.

Hea-vy.

66

Ain't Nobody Gonna Like It

I think we're heading toward a racial train wreck. I'd better be wrong.

The United States is no longer one nation, but three—black, Hispanic, and white—living in uneasy coexistence in the same place. Whites, once dominant, are either no longer able, or no longer willing, to impose a uniform national culture. The two minorities grow in numbers, being encouraged to do so by the federal government, and grow in assertiveness. Can the three meld? Or live in harmony?

The answer, I think, is: Whites and Hispanics, perhaps. Blacks and whites, no. Blacks and Hispanics, no.

Civics courses in high-school hold that America is a melting pot, that different groups eventually blend happily as did the Italians and Irish. Note, though, that previous minorities have been (a) European and (b) sufficiently few to be absorbed. They also wanted to be Americans. These things are not necessarily true of today's minorities.

Further, if you wanted to choose three cultures unlikely to assimilate, our three would be a pretty good choice. Disparate peoples can live in peace, as witness Switzerland, but only if all are thoroughly civilized, law-abiding, and equally well off. That is not the case here.

Look around the world. All of the truly advanced nations, except Japan, are of white European origin. Black nations, without exception, from Africa to Haiti, fall at the dead bottom of civilization. In the United States, blacks also place last, and show few signs of independent progress. Hispanic nations hold the middle ground. This is not a recipe for harmony.

Racial tensions are fairly high today, and growing. After fifty years of attempts to impose integration, American isn't integrated. If the minorities do not assimilate, as they gain power their assertiveness will probably increase. The crucial question becomes: What prospect is there for assimilation before trouble comes—within, say, no more than twenty years?

For blacks, none. They live largely in isolation in vast, utterly segregated, linguistically aberrant, self-sustaining ghettoes. Animosity smolders between them and everyone else. Their economic and academic lassitude prevents easy entry into a techno-industrial society. Explain these failings as you will. They are real, and intractable.

For Hispanics, assimilation is possible but iffy. The stark cultural gap between blacks and whites isn't replicated with browns, nor is the visceral hatred of whites. Mexicans aren't that different from whites—no more so, I'd guess, than Italians or Poles were. Their culture carries a strong European component. Here there is hope. The devil is in the numbers.

If a thousand Hispanics came to the US and dispersed through a city, they would perforce adopt the local culture, intermarry, become Mexican-Americans, and soon simply Americans. By contrast, several million Hispanics concentrated in California may (or, please heaven, may not) become a permanent self-aware nation within a nation, antagonistic to the surrounding country, as blacks have.

Then what?

Blacks and Hispanics approach a quarter of the population, perhaps too many to be absorbed or contained. Large numbers of unassimilable minorities eventually alarm the surrounding population. They also become politically aggressive. They can now make demands of the white population. Whites, especially in regions of concentration, accede. It is hard to say "no" to Hispanics in LA.

Making assimilation more difficult is that neither blacks nor Hispanics perform near the economic or intellectual level of whites. Hispanics may catch up, but probably not soon enough, especially with the constant influx of new uneducated immigrants. The resultant inequality encourages anger.

Which we have in plenty. The hostility of blacks toward whites, though seldom discussed, is powerful. Trouble also brews unnoticed between blacks and Hispanics as Hispanics, more industrious than blacks, begin to outnumber them. Hispanics show up, work hard, follow instructions, and behave well at work. They are fast taking unskilled jobs that blacks once had. Blacks know it. So do Hispanics. Things could get ugly. Racial conflict doesn't necessarily involve whites.

The media carefully avoid publicizing the degree of antagonism, the cost of welfare, or—crucially—the ethnic element in crime, which almost perfectly tracks the black population. (I know, I know: One doesn't say this, but the numbers are there.) Characteristically, when relations between the US and Japan were strained a while back by the rape of Japanese girls in Okinawa by GIs, no photographs of the assailants were published in the mainstream media.

Why the spin? Is there, as some suspect, an organized journalistic conspiracy to control racially inflammatory news? If so, I'm not privy to it. However, journalists see the danger of serious conflict. Maybe their censorship is wise: Accurate reporting would increase tension. Editors know that the United States is not magically immune to the ills of Ireland or Yugoslavia. A repetition of the massive riots of the Sixties by blacks, or the destruction of much of LA by blacks and Hispanics could, given the right spark, become national.

The future? Race is a game of numbers. Birth rates are high among both blacks and Hispanics, low among whites, and everyone is aware of it. Blacks, concentrated in the cities, take over one urban government after another through growing numbers, and know they are doing it.

Hispanics sense that history is on their side, that immigration combined with fertility will allow them to push aside an exhausted white population. "*La reconquista*" is a potent concept. They are beginning to control the Southwest. How bad is this? If relations with whites don't deteriorate, not very bad. If relations go south…

So far, whites have not pushed back. They have no way of doing so. Powerful strictures, supported by the courts, enforced by the media and inculcated by the schools, militate against even discussing race openly— though the taboo wanes. Whites seldom riot, are not yet alarmed enough, have no focus for hostility, no leader, and don't agree that hostility is justified. Yet. But if they begin to feel backed into a corner, if they begin to think in terms of us agin' them, if they foresee becoming a downtrodden minority in their own country. . . they may rebel.

The results would be awful. Whites would win any real confrontation, being far more numerous, richer, and better armed and organized. They also control the food supply, which may not have occurred to angry urban populations. But the country would be wrecked.

Which suggests that we need to think very carefully, and find a way out of the deepening morass while we still can. If we still can.

67

Ill-Breeding,
And A Suggested Cure

I guess if about fifty million people in this country got taken out behind the woodshed, and thrashed within an inch of their lives, we'd have a better place to live. Or at least people with better manners. A size-twelve combat boot would do nicely.

I'm for it.

Whatever happened to common courtesy? Used to be, people had some notion how to behave. They didn't always do it, but they knew they were supposed to. And if they didn't, other folk would let them know they needed to start. People said "Please" and "Thank you" and paid attention to stop lights. When they got onto a bus, they had the grace to let the ones on the bus get off instead of pushing aboard like thirsty cattle. Women mostly acted like ladies and men acted mostly like gentlemen, at least around ladies. Those who didn't were called trash. They were, so it made sense.

The approach worked pretty well. A fellow could spend whole hours without wanting to kill anybody.

I'm not sure what happened, but it sure did. A lot of people today aren't fit to eat at a hog trough. The men swear like doormen in a two-dollar whorehouse, without regard to who's listening. The women talk as badly as the men, and it doesn't sit on'em well. Drivers sail through red lights as if they wanted a mass murder. In Washington people stand right smack in front of the subway door like slabs of fatback so riders can't get off. Then they push their way aboard, the way piglets do when they're headed for the underside of a sow.

These folk truly need to be smacked up-side the head. (I've never been sure how to spell that.)

I've got a cornpone theory about it.

I know. That surprises you.

For a country to be civilized, it's gotta have an agreed-upon idea of how to act, what's good and bad, and what to do to people who don't care. You can get that different ways. The Japanese do it by all being the same culture, except for a few Koreans and Ainu. We did it once by having one dominant culture, with reasonable standards of civilization, and imposing them on everybody else by grim determination and self-confidence.

It was the right thing to do. Society needs to have the gumption to enforce civilization. It's like being a parent. Sometimes you have to say, "No."

Thing is, to impose civilization you gotta know it is civilization. It doesn't do to figure it might be, but you aren't sure, and maybe everything is beautiful in its own way. You have to say, "Nope, that's not beautiful in this town." You have to mean it.

You need to tell people that it's just wrong to squall obscenities in a decent restaurant or sit on three seats in an airport so nobody else can sit down. When a bunch of young blacks on the subway holler Their Word at the tops of their voices, you have to have the moral backbone to call the police, who need to have the authority to say, "Act like human beings, or get off the train. Now."

That's the problem, though. If you won't tell some groups to behave, because they have this or that problem or some hard-luck story, then you can't tell the others either. It doesn't work. The behavior of the worst group always trickles up to everybody else. So now the white kids don't behave either.

You just can't have side-by-side moralities that don't match. Low behavior has advantages for the individual, but disadvantages for society as a whole. We ought to think more about society. "Society," after all, is just an abstractified way of saying "everybody else." Us.

What happened was, I think, is that (don't look too carefully at those verbs) the law got separated from morality. When I was a kid, it wasn't yet. If the corner drugstore had started selling pictures of people making love with dromedaries, the cops would have shut the place down as obscene, and that would have been that. The courts wouldn't have objected. Nobody else would have either. You weren't supposed to sell that stuff. The discussion would have been over.

And everybody knew, and agreed, that you didn't cut in line or urinate on sidewalks in public (a new cultural practice among the ethnically challenged) or just plain be rude and disagreeable.

That was then.

Soon the courts decided that nothing was obscene, especially things that obviously were. This was a huge step. The function of the law had been to uphold the standards of society. Then our courts decided that their function was not to uphold, but to instruct and shepherd, and they had the mentality of a sophomore dorm at Cornell.

Putting it succinctly, the courts made morality illegal.

Then of course people in Hollywood began saturating television and the movies with graphic sex and explicit language and grotesque violence and glorified trashiness. The principle in California is that if you don't have talent, take your pants off.

A problem arose: You can't have people, and in particular children, listening all day to grotesque scatology and watching detailed copulation and expect it not to influence them. Perhaps more important, the attitudes of teenagers and of the ghetto, that "ain't nobody gonna tell me what to do," took over. And nobody could do anything about it. Without the backing of the courts, people could no longer demand civilized comportment.

I don't think we realize how bad things are. We've gotten used to road rage (which is just homicidal bad manners) and surliness and crime and hostility and semiliteracy and self-centeredness. We expect horrific slovenliness from our kids. It seems almost reasonable.

But other places have better sense. Go to Japan. You never find rude people, because there aren't any. The Swiss are unfailingly courteous and honest. You probably can't find a country in Europe as boorish and coarse as we are. Try South Vietnam, for heaven's sake. (I went back for a couple of weeks a few years ago. The Viets were far more pleasant than Americans.)

I think we need to get ball bats, and speak some 'Merkun to low-rent people. This is a country, not a bus station. I think.

Sometimes the correct answer is, "Because we say so."

68

Jawless, Bat-Cagle, And Me

Now, about Cagle. He came, fresh meat out of Danang, onto the eye ward at Bethesda Naval Hospital in the summer of '67, it must have been. He was a handsome, wiry mountain boy out of Tennessee. In a rice paddy he had endeavored to fire a rifle grenade at several of what were then called "gooks," but are now more commonly known as "mathematicians." The grenade exploded on the end of his rifle, and jellied his eyes.

For about three days he lay curled in a ball on his rack, in those blue pajamas they gave us, saying nothing. New blind guys always did that. Then he began to pull out of it. They made them tough in Tennessee.

It turned out Cagle was a natural socialite, connoisseur of poontang, and raconteur extraordinary. He fit right into the life of the ward, which was fairly strange.

There was Jawless, who had taken an AK round in the jaw at Plei Ku, shattering the bone, which had to be removed. While the doctors looked for a replacement jaw, he had an NG tube coming out of his nose so he could eat nasty mush, and talked like he was gargling Silly Putty. Rooster was a jarhead whose retinas had begun peeling for unknown reasons at Khe Sanh. And McGoo, a tall doofus squid who had done something heroic on a PBR—that's Patrol Boat, River—and gotten both a major medal and shot up doing it. He wore thick glasses like glass base-plates for a mortar. Navy guys are weird.

An open-bay ward wasn't a bad place to be. It was certainly better than where we'd been. Washington was nearby, bursting with beer and women. Cagle liked both. We started taking him downtown to go sightseeing. He liked sightseeing. We'd take him down to the Mall in the afternoon and point him at the Washington Monument. Cagle would say, "Oh man. God that's something. My brain-housing unit can barely wrap around it. Out-blanking-standing."

The tourists could tell he was blind as three bats in a leather bag and thought we were terrible to be tormenting him that way. One time we pointed him at a tree, and told him it was the Capitol. He went into raptures about how he recognized all the Senators coming out. The tourists weren't sure what to make of that. Jawless and his tube didn't help them decide.

Anyway that night we came back through Friendship Heights, the closest the bus came to the hospital, and we were several sheets to the wind, and probably the blankets and pillowcases too. It was dark and rainy. We ducked for shelter into a doorway and discovered a high school couple trying to cuddle there. They really didn't want four shot-up jarheads without jaws and other parts to share their doorway. But it was raining.

The guy kid had one of those red soft-cotton fender covers mechanics use to keep from scratching up your car. He gave it to us so we could use it for an umbrella and go away. Especially go away. We did.

I forget whose idea it was, but somebody noticed that the fender cover looked like a cape. So we got a marker pen and wrote, "Bat Cagle" on it, and Cagle wore it with his blue PJs. He also had a pair of jungle boots without laces that he slopped around in, just for the hell of it. Discipline wasn't too bad on the ward. The doctors realized we needed a little room to reassemble ourselves. And as Cagle said, "What are they going to do? Send me to Vietnam?"

That would have been the end of it if we hadn't found somewhere a garrison cap—the hat with the visor and the cloth cover on top. If you take the cloth off, there's a little white wire pole with what looks like a halo attached. We gave it to Cagle and let him feel it. He sort of liked it. His own halo. He thought maybe he could deceive women with it.

For some time nothing happened. We took Cagle to parties arranged by Senators who didn't give a damn about us but thought giving us parties might get votes. We didn't care. Beer was beer. The Senators always stocked the pond with college girls. Cagle could work the disabled-hero routine to get more poontang than any six guys needed. He had the drawl and the aw-shucks yes-ma'am cute-and-dumb-as-seven-foxes patter and looked like Elvis.

Well, one day they said there was going to be a huge inspection of the ward. The nurses went into a prevent defense, cleaning everything up. For days it went on. They told us we were supposed to stand at the end of our racks and come to attention on command. I'm not sure we got into the spirit of the thing.

The big day came. We stood at the end of our racks. The commanding admiral's entourage swept regally into the ward—the big guy himself, a cloud of friendly low-ranking nurses, and the head of the nursing corps. This was before many heterosexual women went into the career military, and the head nurse looked like a front lineman mixed with a pit bull.

So help me, Cagle was there in blue pajamas and the Bat Cape, in the unlaced jungles, with the black visor and his halo on its little pole. And holding his white cane. I guess he didn't care any more.

As they came by, Cagle snapped up the cane a in a precise rifle salute. It was awesome. The admiral took one look at this apparition, said, "At ease," and swept by. He probably had a sense of humor, and anyway what was he going to do? Put a blind Marine in irons? It was the wrong hill to die on.

The young nurses smiled despite themselves, since Cagle really did look like Elvis. The head nurse glared hatred. She was ready to eat a doorknob. She wanted to stop and kill him, but the admiral wasn't in the killing mood and so she had to go with him.

Cagle was our hero. Someday I'll tell you how Jawless got another jaw.

69

The Great Possum-Squashing And Beer Storm of 1962

You gotta understand that we were stone crazy back in 1962, in King George County, Virginia. The county was mostly woods. We were mostly country kids. Unisex hadn't hit in those days, nor sensitivity, and certainly not judgement. High school boys burned rubber along the winding forest roads in smoking jalopies that usually ran on a few cylinders less than they had. We drank beer, pulled on cheroots hanging low and sulky the way James Dean did it, and talked of cars and poontang. Some few of us, not to be named here, occasionally fired out the window with a twelve-gauge at cats. Usually I missed.

Anyway, we figured there was nothing in life but engines, guns, brew, and girls. And fishing poles. Even today, I'm persuaded that if there is, there shouldn't be.

As they say in Alabama, we didn't have the sense God give a crab apple. You know something? I'm glad we didn't. I've never done anything sensible that was fully satisfying.

Anyway in tenth grade I drove a '53 Chevy the color of dirt. (This all has a point. I think. Involving possums.) It cornered like a giraffe with its feet roped together and topped out at eighty down a sheer cliff, but it ran. That was enough. Our standards were low. If a car didn't have rod knock, we thought something was wrong with it.

The country boys were my friends, because they had a pleasant suicidal elan that bored me less than other things. There was a kid we called Itchy, because if he was out hunting and saw a bug crawling up a plant, he'd give it both barrels. He wasn't a repressed killer or anything. It was just how he responded to bugs. I understand he later became a sane adult. We all knew he'd come to a bad end.

This isn't very coherent, but we're getting there. Patience.

So one Saturday night Itch and Jimbo and Bobby, I'll call 'em, were out motivating along Route 218 with me in the '53. It could have been 2 a.m. The road was narrow, and wound through the forest like a python with epilepsy. Jimbo was a muscular farm boy with an IQ approximating his shoe size. Bobby, like me, was a mathematician's kid from the Naval Research Lab in the county. He was blond and skinny and looked like a tubular Viking.

Trees sailed by in the headlights and we had a case of Budweiser. Drinking and driving at age sixteen wasn't a good idea. On the other hand, if any of us had encountered a good idea, we would have reported it to the police. The air was chilly with October. We felt free and wild, young males in the night. Conversation was articulate and sophisticated:

"Gittin' any strange?"

"Here and there." Lying is easier when not enshrouded by details.

"Would be strange if you got it. Gimme another beer."

In the midst of this philosophy, a possum scurried onto the road. In the headlights it looked like a vast rat that needed braces. I hit the brakes, having nothing against possums.

Not fast enough. *Blub-blup.*

Jimbo thought this was splendid, exciting, as if we had found Moby Dick crouching in a duck blind.

"*Back up! Back up, Ricky! Let's look!*" he hollered. He had curious tastes in things to look at. In those days I was called Ricky.

We backed up until the steaming carcass lay in the headlights and got out, leaving the car running, and walked over to it. Yellow teeth snarled up from mangled fur. If anything ever needed braces, that possum did. For a moment we stood there, listening to the engine whuffing behind us. Then, without consultation, we all peed on the beast. I don't know why. We didn't think it was funny. It just seemed...right. Maybe the beer inspired us. Maybe we were marking our territory. (A flat possum?)

I don't recommend it. I'm just telling you what happened.

Anyway, things proceeded to get strange, and they were starting from a pretty good baseline. Jimbo decided he wanted to ride in the trunk. The point was hard to argue. I mean, who else could tell what he wanted? There in the star-sprinkled night, trees everywhere, possum cooling, I opened the trunk and Jimbo sat, beer in hand, on the spare tire. He looked like Buddha with muscles. That too seemed right. It probably wasn't.

Then Bob decided *he* wanted to ride on the roof. This wasn't smart. Neither was Bob, which preserved symmetry. (I think he went to Princeton, which proves it.)

We'd had an awful lot of beer. I thought about the roof. Everybody had to be somewhere, I decided. Any fool knew that. Onto the roof Bob went.

We actually drove off like that. How any of us survived to adulthood is a mystery. Itch curled up on the seat next to me. I seem to remember that he was muttering about alligators, but I could be wrong. In any event, I'm pretty sure we didn't have any alligators. We throbbed along very slowly, since the driver had, barely, sense enough to know Bob might fall off.

Occasionally I checked to see whether he was still on the roof. I could tell he was because his fingers hung over the edge of the windshield. Jimbo whooped and hollered in the trunk.

A tremendous downpour began. The windshield just streamed water. I turned on the wipers. Itchy began muttering more enthusiastically, but less articulately. I glanced at him. And noticed that it wasn't raining on his side of the car.

That was odd, I thought. My experience had been that storms weren't so local. They usually got both sides of a car. It was like a rule.

Further, the road was dry. As storms went, this one was on the peculiar side.

As it turned out, Bob was holding his beer by the wrong end on the roof, and it was running down the windshield. I yelled at him to stop.

I don't know what to tell you. It's how things were. And, when you get down to it, I wish they still were.

About the Author

Fred, a keyboard mercenary with a disorganized past, has worked on staff for *Army Times, The Washingtonian, Soldier of Fortune, Federal Computer Week,* and *The Washington Times.* He has been published in *Playboy, Soldier of Fortune, The Wall Street Journal, The Washington Post, Harper's, National Review, Signal, Air&Space,* and suchlike. He has worked as a police writer, technology editor, military specialist, and authority on mercenary soldiers.

As he tells it, he was born in 1945 in Crumpler, West Virginia, a coal camp near Bluefield. His father was a mathematician then serving in the Pacific aboard the destroyer USS Franks, which he described as a wallowing antique serving more as a distraction than a menace to the Japanese.

His paternal grandfather was dean, and professor of mathematics and classical languages, at Hampden-Sydney College, a small and (then, and perhaps now) quite good liberal arts school in southwest Virginia. His maternal grandfather was a doctor in Crumpler. (When someone got sick on the other side of the mountain, the miners would put Doctor Reed in a coal car and take him under the mountain. His, says Fred, was a fairly robust conception of a house call.) Fred says his family for many generations were among the most literate, the most productive, and the dullest people in the South. Presbyterians.

After the war he lived as a navy brat here and there: San Diego, Mississippi, the Virginia suburbs of Washington, Alabama, and briefly in Farmville, Virginia, while his father went on active duty for the Korean War as an artillery spotter. He describes himself as a voracious and undiscriminating reader and a terrible student. By age eleven he had an eye for elevation and windage with a BB gun that would have awed a missile engineer, and had become a mad scientist. He thinks he was ten when he discovered the formula for thermite in the Britannica at Athens College in Athens, Alabama, stole the ingredients from the college chemistry laboratory, and ignited a mound of perfectly adequate thermite in the prize frying pan of the mother of his friend Perry, whose father was the college president. The resulting six-inch hole in the frying pan was hard to explain.

He went to high school in King George County, Virginia, where he remembers being the kid other kids weren't supposed to play with. He spent his time in canoeing, shooting, drinking unwise but memorable amounts of beer with the local country boys, and attempting to be a French rake "with less success than I will admit to." He reports driving his 1953 Chevy, the Pluke Bucket, "in a manner that, if you are a country boy, I don't have to describe, and if you aren't, you wouldn't believe anyway."

As usual he was a woeful student, asserting that if he and his friend Butch hadn't found the mimeograph stencil for the senior Government exam in the school's Dempster Dumpster, he would still be in high school. He surprised himself and his teachers by being a National Merit Finalist, thus learning of the redemptive powers of standardized tests.

After two years at Hampden-Sydney, where he worked on a split major in chemistry and biology with an eye to oceanography, he was bored. After spending the summer thumbing across the continent and down into Mexico, hopping freight trains up and down the eastern seaboard, and generally confusing himself with Jack Kerouac, he enlisted in the Marines. He thought that it would be more interesting than stirring unpleasant glops in the laboratory. He reports that it was.

On returning from Vietnam with a lot of stories, as well as a Purple Heart and more shrapnel in his face eyes than he says he really wanted, he graduated from Hampden-Sydney with lousy grades. He holds a bachelor-of-science degree with a major in history and a minor in computers. Again to the surprise of all, he says, his GREs were in the 99th percentile.

The years from 1970 to 1973 he spent in disreputable pursuits, his favorite. Wandering through Europe, Asia, and Mexico.

When the 1973 war broke out in the Mid-East, Fred says he decided he ought to do something respectable, thought that journalism was, and told the editor of his home-town paper, "Hi! I want to be a war correspondent." This, he says, was a sufficiently damn-fool thing to do that the paper let him go, probably to see what would happen. "Writing," he discovered, "was the only thing I was good for. It's the moral equivalent of being a wino, but you don't have to carry a brown-paper bag."

He spent the last year of the Vietnam War War between Phnom Penh and Saigon, living in "slums that would have horrified a New York alley cat," and left each city the evacuation. After the fall of Saigon he returned and studied Chinese while waiting for the next war, which didn't come. For a year he worked in Boulder, Colorado, on the staff of Soldier of Fortune magazine, "half zoo and half asylum," with the intention of writing a book about it. Publishing houses said, yes, Fred, this is great stuff, but you are obviously making it up. He insists that wasn't. Playboy eventually published it, making Fred extremely persona non grata at Soldier of Fortune.

Having gotten married somewhere along the way for reasons he says he can no longer remember, he is now the happily divorced father of the World's Finest Daughters, lives in Arlington, Virginia, and work as, among other things, a law-enforcement columnist for the Washington Times, and a contributor to Signal magazine ("encryption and weird radar.") The income, he says, allows him to take trips abroad, to ride around in police cars with the siren howling, and kick in the doors of drug dealers. His hobbies are wind surfing, scuba, listening to blues, swing-dancing in dirt bars, associating with the intelligently disreputable, weight-lifting, and people of the other gender.